First Time Home Buying 101

Dedicated to all First-Time Home Buyers

About the Author

Shashank Shekhar is widely regarded as "Bay Area's First Time Home Buyer Expert". He regularly writes about lending and real estate industry on his blog post www.LendingExpertBlog.com. Shashank is also a sought after industry speaker and has been featured on various TV & radio Shows.

He has an MBA in Marketing. Shashank's business philosophy is to "create raving fans" out of all his clients and referral partners. He achieves this by offering "legendary service" that is reflected in 100% satisfaction record of his clients.

Shashank's more than 9 years of lending business experience includes working for GE Money in mid level management and working for a start-up mortgage origination company as Director of Product Management. He is currently the CEO of Arcus Lending, Inc. a mortgage brokerage company based in San Jose, CA that he founded in 2008.

He is a licensed California Real Estate Broker #01734034 and can be reached via email at Shashank@ArcusLending.com.

Disclaimer

Please note the information contained within this book is for educational purposes only. Every attempt has been made to provide accurate, up to date, reliable and complete information. No warranties of any kind are expressed or implied. Readers acknowledge that the author is not engaging in rendering legal, financial or professional advice.

By reading this book, the reader agrees that under no circumstances are we responsible for any losses, direct or indirect, that are incurred as a result of use of the information contained within this document, including - but not limited to errors, omissions, or inaccuracies.

Introduction

At the time of writing this book nearly half of home sales were being made by first-time purchasers. In fact, 47% of all Americans who purchased homes in 2009 had not owned one during the previous three years, according to National Association of Realtors (NAR). That was up from 41% of sales in 2008 and 36% in 2006. In 2009, there were 2.3 to 2.4 million first-time home buyers.

In my specialty, as a First Time Home Buyer Expert, I speak to a lot of people every day. A large portion of them are people who are either in the process of buying their first home, contemplating the issue or flat out not sure if they should buy one. It does not matter what category they fall in, they still have a lot of questions about different stages of the process. First time home buying is a special occasion in everyone's life. But because of the complexities around it, most people approach it with a mix of fear, anxiety and uncertainty.

I wrote this book with the sole purpose of making the process easier and more predictable. I do not want lack of knowledge to come in your way of not buying your own home. I have tried to demystify the entire process by avoiding the jargon as much as possible. The book first helps you in deciding whether you are ready to buy or not and then gives a step by step instruction on what you can expect along the process should you decide to buy. My favorite part of the book is the last chapter where I interview 7 First-Time Home Buyers.

Once you have read the book, let me know if it was able to meet its goals. Also, if you can think of some other topics and/or questions that the book did not answer, feel free to let me know. I will try to include them in my future editions.

Join the conversation at www.FirstTimeHomeBuying101.com and/or the book's Facebook Fan Page at www.Facebook.com/FirstTimeHomeBuying 101.

Best wishes

Shashank

Table of Contents

"The strength of a nation is derived from the integrity of its homes."

Confucius (China's most famous teacher, Philosopher and Political Theorist)

The State of Real Estate

Over the last few years, home prices have corrected and become more affordable. While that's good news for potential buyers, it has overshadowed the long-term appreciation of a home's value. The reality is, despite market ups and downs between 1950 and 2002, US home prices appreciated at an annual growth rate of 4.8%. Even if you calculate a modest appreciation of 3%, a home purchased today for $150,000 will grow in value to $364,000 over 30 years.

At the time of writing this book nearly half of home sales were being made by first-time purchasers. In fact, 47% of all Americans who purchased homes in 2009 had not owned one during the previous three years. That was up from 41% of sales in 2008 and 36% in 2006. In 2009 there were 2.3 to 2.4 million First-time home buyers. (Data source – National Association of Realtors)

The home prices had gone so low that investors are being able to rent out homes for enough to cover their mortgage payments and renters can now buy homes at almost same payment as rent. That's why we are seeing wave of people snapping bargain houses. We have already started to see the prices stabilizing in some areas and even inching up.

National Association of Realtor's Chief Economist Lawrence Yun recently remarked – "As inventories continue to decline and balance is gradually restored between buyers and sellers, we should reach self-sustaining housing conditions and firming home prices in most areas around the middle of 2010."

The low mortgage rates have been a huge contributor to the revival of Real Estate market. The table below illustrates average mortgage interest rates on conforming loans – Loan Amount 417,000 or lower (Source – Freddie Mac)

	2000	2005	2006	2007	2008	2009
30 Year Fixed	8.05	6.27	6.14	6.34	6.03	5.04
5 Year ARM	n/a	5.32	6.08	6.07	5.74	4.75

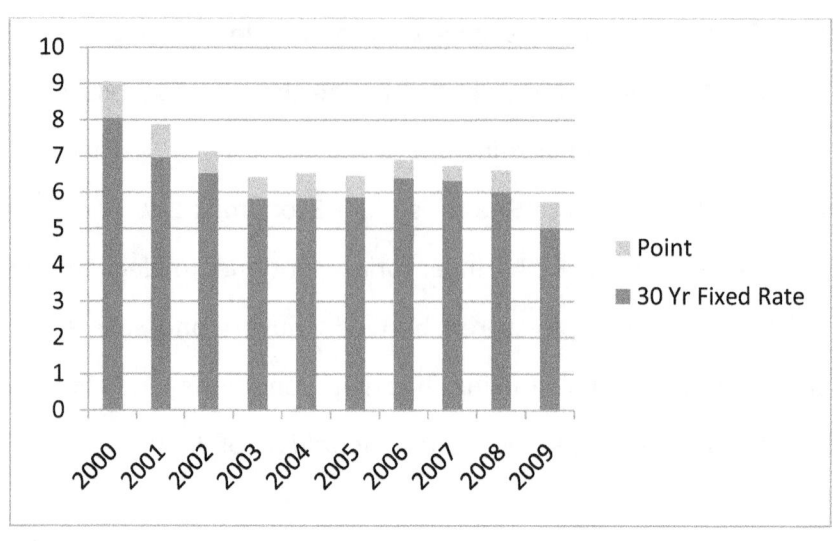

What does it mean for you if you are currently renting?

Affordability Index:

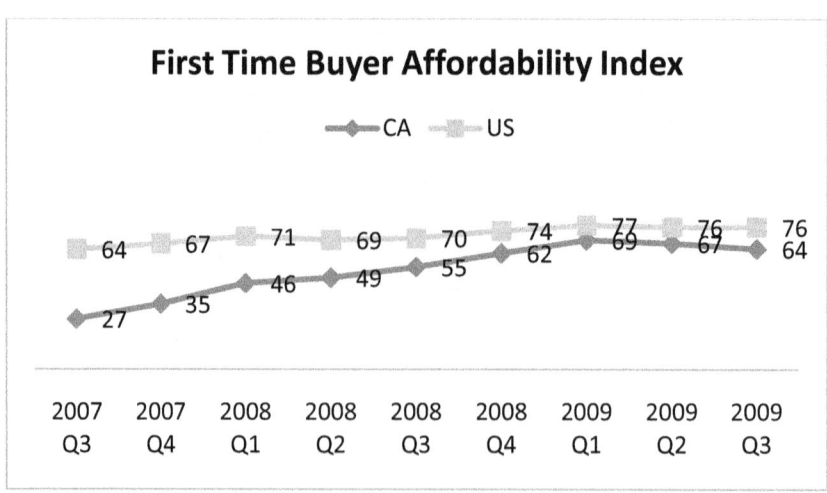

With 15%-25% drop in property prices and 75-100 basis points drop in average interest rates, more renters can now afford to buy a home compared to couple of years back. Affordability index measures the percentage of homes sold that a median income family in a metropolitan area can buy. At the end of 2006 First-Time buyer affordability index was in the low 20s in California, but jumped to mid 60s for most part of 2009 (Source – California Association of Realtors). This means that now almost 2 in 3 households can afford to buy houses in California wherein earlier it was 1 in 4 households. To read more about the First-Time Home Buyer Affordability Index you can read one of my blog posts at http://lendingexpertblog.com/blogs/?p=722.

"If I were asked to name the chief benefit of the house, I would say: the house shelters daydreaming, the house protects the dreamer, the house allows one to dream in peace."

Gaston Bachelard

The Benefits of Home Ownership

 Recently, the National Association Of Realtors® surveyed First-time homebuyers to find out what they considered to be most important in the purchase of their homes. The largest percentage, 62 percent, considered the mere ownership of a home as the most important reason to buy. Change in family situation (8 percent), Affordability of homes (10 percent), First Time Home buyer tax credit (8 percent), Job related relocation (2 percent), Establish household (2 percent) and Desire for larger homes (2 percent) were other reasons cited for buying homes.

For you it could an asset, an investment or an American Dream. Home ownership is the greatest American Dream, is it not? Even in this era of record foreclosures, the percentage of U.S. households that now own, rather than rent, is an all time high. It's not a surprise given several benefits of homeownership.

Rent vs. Buy

No Matter what you are currently paying for rent, your total cash outlay over a period of several years will probably add up to a much higher total than you may have realized.

Compare a renter who pays $1800/month with 5% increase in rent every year and a homeowner who buys a $500,000 home and the home appreciates at 5% every year.

	Rent Payment	Property Appreciation
Year 1	21600	25000
Year 2	22680	26250
Year 3	23814	27562
Year 4	25004	28940
Year 4	26254	30387
Total	119352	138139

In the above example a renter ends up paying ~$120,000 in rents over a 5 year period while a homeowner ends up building ~$140,000 in equity. These numbers may or may not be true in all real life scenarios, but it gives you an idea.

Tax Benefits

When you are figuring out how much you can afford to commit to monthly mortgage payments, do not forget about the tax benefits. The US government allows tax incentives that make it possible for many homeowners to exceed the standard yearly deduction. The following three components of your home mortgage are tax deductible:

- Interest on your home mortgage.
- Property taxes.
- Loan points for a purchase mortgage

Don't Wait for a Tax Return – Get That Money Now

The IRS allows you to increase the number of dependants on your W-4 withholding form, meaning that less will be withheld for taxes from each paycheck. After you buy your house, I strongly suggest you do that. This lets you have more money in each paycheck instead of "loaning" the money to the IRS and having to wait for a refund.

But don't go overboard. You should only lessen the periodic tax withholding to match the expected refund. This way you are taking your refund as you go; Instead of letting the IRS hold on to it. Consider visiting the IRS Withholdings Calculator to see how a change will impact your paycheck. Just visit www.irs.gov and type "Withholding Calculator" into the search bar at the top.

In the early years of a typical mortgage a large portion of your monthly payment goes towards paying mortgage interest. That means as a homeowner your annual taxable income can be substantially reduced if you owned a house.

Homeowners Have More Stability

Owners typically stay in their home 12 years whereas renters stay no more than 3 years. Remaining in one neighborhood for several years lets you and your family establish lasting friendships, and offers your children the benefit of educational continuity.

Appreciation of Property

As home prices have fallen precipitously in today's tough economy, the basis for realizing appreciation in future years is very strong. Historically, even with other periods of declining value, home prices have exceeded consumer inflation. From 1972 through 2005, home prices increased on average 6.5%, according to the National Association of Realtors®.

Forced Saving

The monthly payment helps in repayment of the principal amount, thereby increasing the equity of the house. Also when you sell you can generally take up to $250,000 ($500,000 for married couple) as gain without owing any federal income tax.

Increased Net Worth

Few things have a greater impact on net worth than owning a home. In a comparison of renters versus homeowners, the Federal Reserve Board of Consumer Finance found that the average net worth of renters was just $4,000 compared to homeowners at $184,400.

Average net worth of homeowners vs. renters

Annual income	Owners	Renters
$80,000 and up	$451,200	$87,400
$50,000 to $79,999	$194,610	$25,000
$30,000 to $49,999	$126,500	$10,600
$16,000 to $29,999	$112,600	$4,240
Under $16,000	$73,000	$500

Source: VIP Forum, Federal Reserve Board, MSN Money.com

Positive Environments for Families

Children of homeowners are 59% more likely to become homeowners. Their children are also 25% more likely to graduate from high school and 16% more likely to graduate from college.

Having a place you can call your own

There can be no other benefit that can beat the emotional satisfaction of home ownership. Whether it's having the nicest lawn on the block or having your own backyard and garage or being able to color the walls the way you want, is so much more fun than renting.

Special $8000 Federal Tax credit

 President Obama recently signed a bill that extends the tax credit for first-time homebuyers (FTHBs) into the first half of 2010. This program had been scheduled to expire on November 30, 2009.

In addition to extending the tax credit of up to $8,000 through June 30, 2010, the extension measure also opens up opportunities for others who are not buying a home for the first time.

So Who Gets What? The program that has existed for FTHBs remains intact with the one exception that more people are now eligible based on an increase in the amount of income someone may now earn.

Additionally, the program now gives those who already own a residence some additional reasons to move to a new home. This incentive comes in the form of a tax credit of up to $6,500 for qualified purchasers who have owned and occupied a primary residence for a period of five consecutive years during the last eight years.

Deadlines: In order to qualify for the credit, all contracts need to be in effect no later than April 30, 2010 and close no later than June 30, 2010.

Higher Income Caps in Effect: The amount of income someone can earn and qualify for the full amount of the credit has been increased.

Single tax filers who earn up to $125,000 are eligible for the total credit amount. Those who earn more than this cap can receive a partial credit. However, single filers who earn $145,000 and above are ineligible.

Joint filers who earn up to $225,000 are eligible for the total credit amount. Those who earn more than this cap can receive a partial credit. However, joint filers who earn $245,000 and above are ineligible.

Maximum Purchase Price: Qualifying buyers may purchase a property with a maximum sales price of $800,000.

"The foundations of civilization are no stronger and no more enduring than the corporate integrity of the homes on which they rest. If the home deteriorates, civilization will crumble and fall."

Billy Graham, American Evangelist

Are you ready to buy?

As covered in the preceding chapter this could be a great time to buy and there are many advantages of home ownerships. But it's not all roses and peach. Before taking probably the biggest financial decision of your life so far, you should do your homework. If you don't do your homework, your dream can very well turn into your greatest financial nightmare.

True cost of homeownership

Sometimes people make the decision of buying based on simply the mortgage payment vs. the rent that they are paying. I cannot tell you how wrong they are.

Mortgage payment is just one component of total cost of homeownership. On an average you need to add another 25-40 percent to get more realistic total monthly cost. Let's take an example. Say you are buying a house worth $450,000 and putting 10% i.e. $45,000 as down payment. Your monthly mortgage payment at 5.5% is $2,300. But your total housing payment would be ~$3,000 after including property taxes, homeowner's insurance and mortgage insurance payment. As you can see your total housing payment is 30% more than your mortgage payment.

And that's not it. If you were buying a condominium or a town home you would also pay a Home Owner's Association fees. And we are still not done. Let's not forget all the costs of keeping the house running. You need to cover repair and upkeep costs for your home. You should allocate about $100 a month for this "repair fund".

Get your finances in order

I personally recommend the below mentioned 4 step process to my clients:

Step 1 – Figure out how much buying a home in your estimated price range will really cost you monthly, including all the expenses.

Step 2 – Subtract your current monthly rent from the total figure you came up with in Step 1. For example, if your rent is $2000 and your monthly homeownership cost is $3,000 that is a difference of $1000 per month.

Step 3 – Set up a new bank account. On the first day of each month – you are to deposit whatever the difference is between your current rent and what your projected homeownership costs would be; in our example, you would deposit $1000 into the account.

Step 4 – You are to do this every month for 6 months. If you are late in your payments, or if you feel stressed out trying to make the payments, you should take this as a sign that you may not be financially ready to become a homeowner.

Whether you take this recommended test and failed or whether you don't want to take this test at all, below are some ways in which you can get your finances in order before starting on your home search.

Reduce your debt/expenses – While majority of expenses like Rent, Tuition, and Utilities etc. can't be done away with, but little expenses add up. Try writing down everything you spend for couple of months and you would notice some expenses that you can cut down on. Some of the expenses that you should be able to cut down are dining out, movies, shopping etc. Also it's a good idea to use coupons and research to find bargains when you are shopping.

Develop a budgeting habit – After you have written all your expenses for couple of months, you would get a fair idea of where your money is being spent. And then create a budget that you would like to stick to. Make sure to factor in unexpected expense like Illnesses, Car repair etc.

Another way to develop a budget is to have a realistic savings target. Subtract your targeted savings from your take home monthly income and spend only what is left.

Save for down payment and reserves – Budgeting and cutting down on expenses will help you save for down payment of your home if you haven't already done that. While saving money for down payment, make sure you also save for 3-6 months of extra reserves to cover all your housing payment to have a cushion for any extenuating circumstances like a Job loss or an illness etc.

Keep a tab on bills – Know when your bills are due and pay them on time to prevent any late charges or additional interest cost. Have one person in the house assigned for this job. Also consider making payments via auto-debit program wherever possible. Make sure to check with your creditor and financial institution that they are not charging an additional fee for this service.

Now that I have walked you through all the issues to consider, I want to put everything in perspective. Homeownership is a great achievement and a terrific investment. Just make sure you can afford it before you can take the plunge.

"You are a King by your own fireside, as much as any monarch in his throne."

Miguel De Cervantes

Step-By-Step Walkthrough

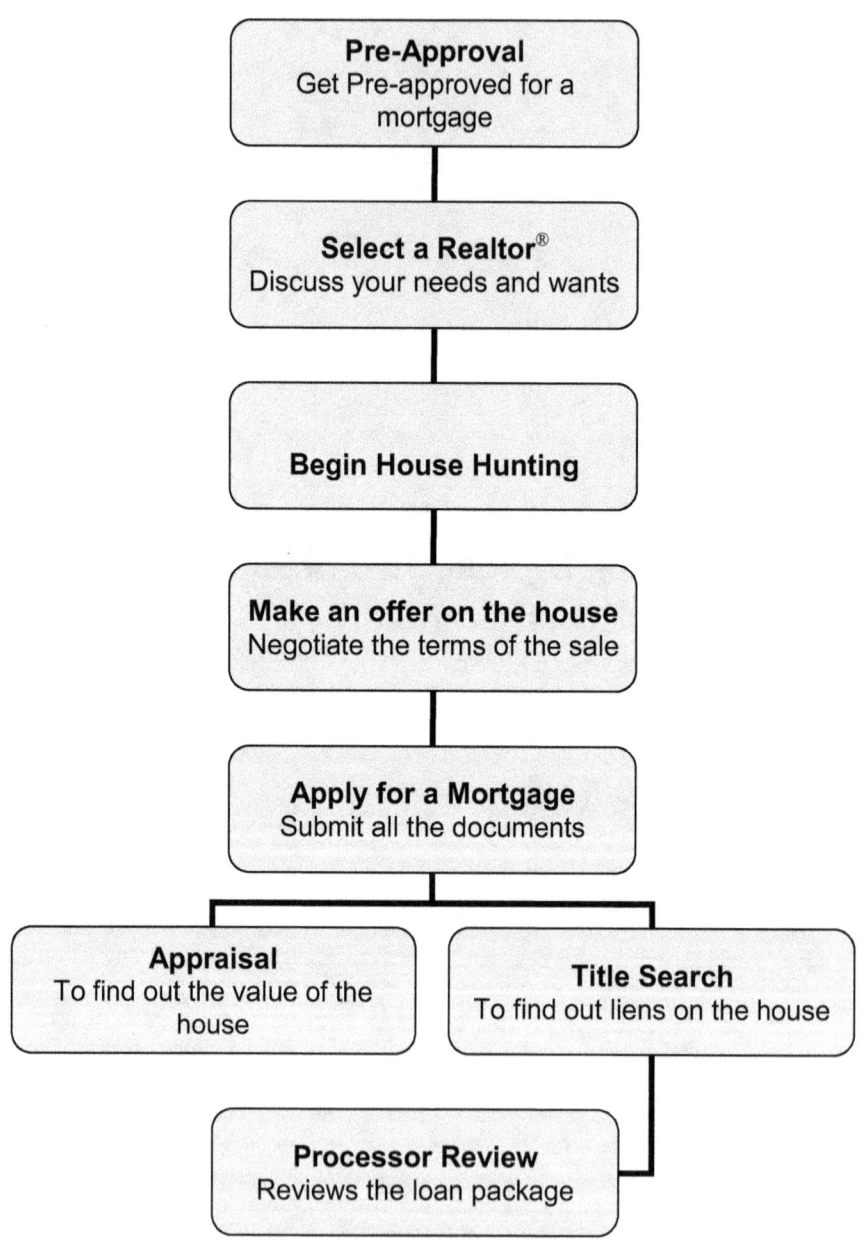

Pre-Approval
Get Pre-approved for a mortgage

Select a Realtor®
Discuss your needs and wants

Begin House Hunting

Make an offer on the house
Negotiate the terms of the sale

Apply for a Mortgage
Submit all the documents

Appraisal
To find out the value of the house

Title Search
To find out liens on the house

Processor Review
Reviews the loan package

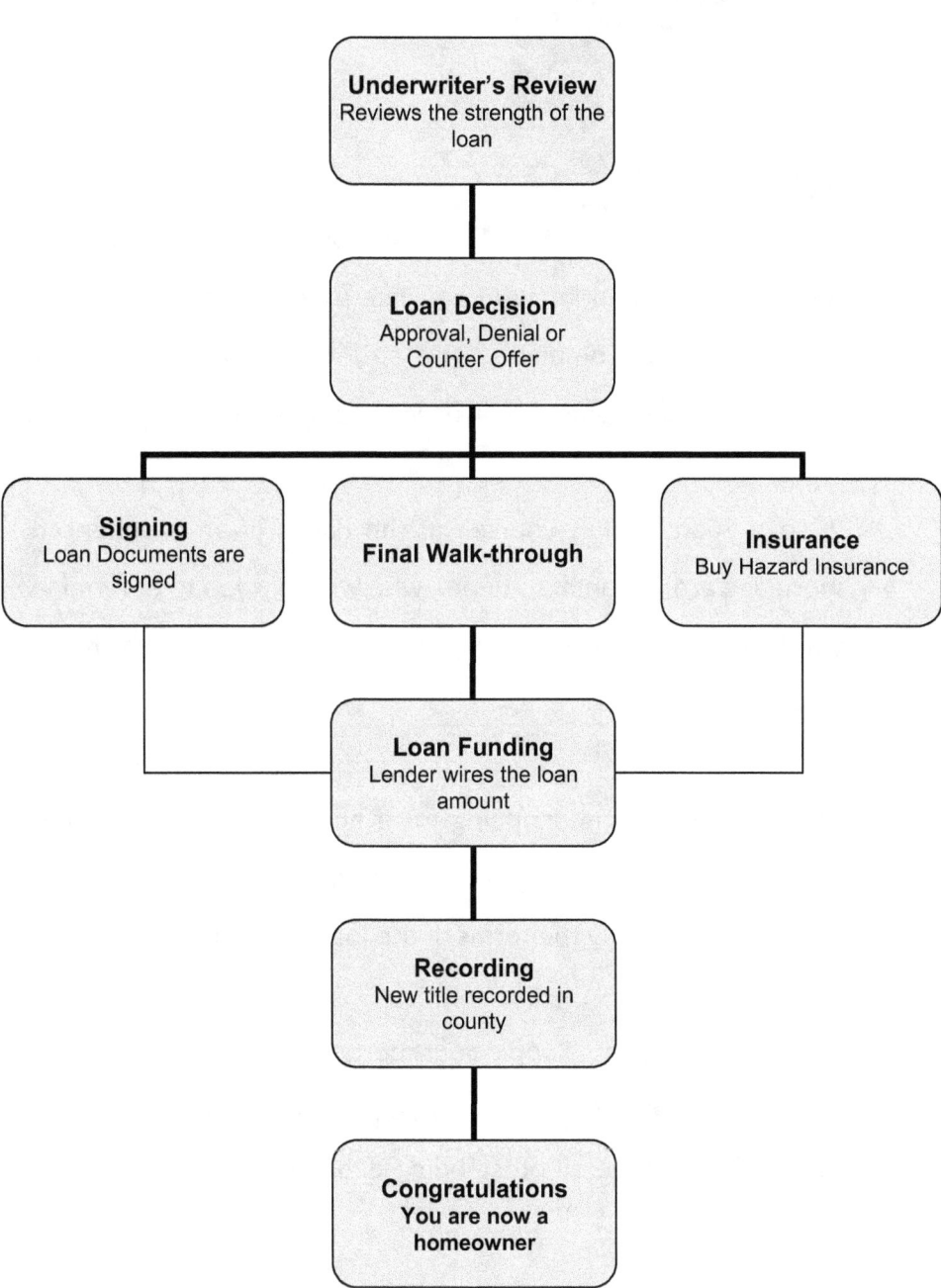

 1. Pre-approval – Get pre-approved for a mortgage and know in advance exactly how much house you can afford. Completing this step will also increase your negotiating power since you'll be viewed as a "cash buyer".

2. Loan Search – Put yourself in the hands of an experienced mortgage professional, someone who will help you to determine which financing options best suit your needs today and in the future.

3. The Hunt – Begin shopping for a house. Once you find the right one, the terms of the sale will be negotiated, including the price and potentially the terms of the loan being sought.

4. Loan Application – Supply your mortgage professional with all required information, and try to be as accurate as possible. It's essential to include all outstanding debts as well as assets and income.

5. Documentation – Submit the proper paperwork supporting your application to your loan professional.

F A Q What are the documents required for a mortgage loan process?

Commonly requested items include

Wage Earner:

- ✓ Last 2 year W2s
- ✓ 2 most recent Pay Stubs
- ✓ 2 most recent all bank statements, 401(K) statements etc.
- ✓ If Bonus/Commission income – Last 2 year Tax returns

Self Employed:

- ✓ 2 Most Recent all bank statements
- ✓ Last 2 year Tax returns
- ✓ Last Quarter P&L statement

6. Appraisal – Lenders require an appraisal on all home sales. By knowing the true value of the home, the borrower is protected from overpaying.

7. Title Search – This is the time when any liens against the property are discovered. A lien may have been placed on a

property to ensure payment of outstanding debts by the owner. All liens must be cleared before a transaction can be completed.

8. Termite Inspection – Most purchase loans require an inspection for termite and water damage. Some problems may need to be repaired before finalizing the sale.

9. Processor's Review – All pertinent information will be packaged by your mortgage professional and sent to the lending underwriter, including any explanations that may be needed, such as reasons for derogatory credit.

10. Underwriter's Review – Based on the information put together by the loan professional, the underwriter makes the final decision regarding whether a loan is approved.

11. Mortgage Insurance – Many lenders require private mortgage insurance when borrowers put down less than 20 percent on a loan. If that is the case an underwriter from the Mortgage Insurance company may review the loan package independently of the lender.

12. Approval, Denial or Counter Offer – The loan can either get approved, denied or approved subject to certain conditions e.g. In order to approve a loan, the lender may ask the borrowers to

put more money down to improve the debt-to-income ratio. The borrower may also need a bigger down payment if the property appraises for less than the purchase price.

13. Insurance – Lenders require fire and hazard insurance on the replacement value of the structure. Flood insurance will also be required if the property is located in a flood zone. In California and some other states, some lenders may require earthquake insurance in some areas.

14. Signing – During this step, final loan and escrow documents are signed.

15. Funding – At this point, the lender will send a wire or check for the amount of the loan to the title company.

16. Closing – Documents transferring title will now be officially recorded by the County Recorder.

17. Congratulations, you are now a homeowner!

"We shape our dwellings, and afterwards our dwellings shape us."

Winston Churchill

How to choose your Home Buying Team

Choosing a Real Estate Agent

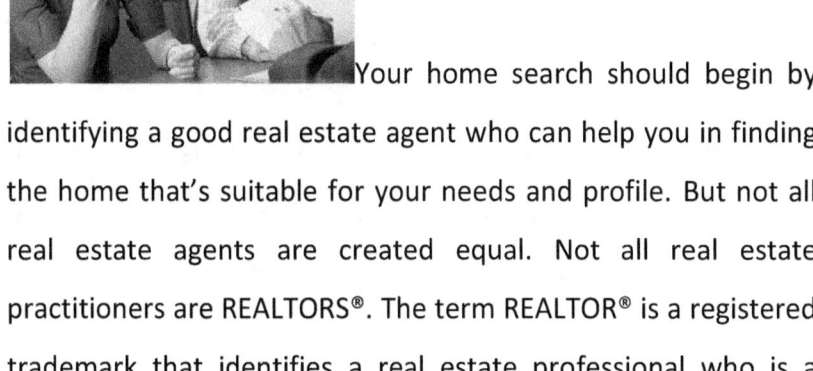 Your home search should begin by identifying a good real estate agent who can help you in finding the home that's suitable for your needs and profile. But not all real estate agents are created equal. Not all real estate practitioners are REALTORS®. The term REALTOR® is a registered trademark that identifies a real estate professional who is a member of the NATIONAL ASSOCIATION of REALTORS® and subscribes to its strict Code of Ethics.

*Here are five reasons why it pays to work with a REALTOR®

1. You'll have an expert to guide you through the process. Buying a home usually requires disclosure forms, inspection reports, mortgage documents, insurance policies, deeds, and multi-page settlement statements. A knowledgeable expert will help you prepare the best deal, and avoid delays or costly mistakes.

2. Get objective information and opinions. REALTORS® can provide local community information on utilities, zoning, schools, and more. They'll also be able to provide objective information about each property. A professional will be able to help you answer these two important questions: Will the property provide the environment I want for a home? Second, will the property have resale value when I am ready to sell?

3. Find the best property out there. Sometimes the property you are seeking is available but not actively advertised in the market, and it will take some investigation by your REALTOR® to find all available properties.

4. Benefit from their negotiating experience. There are many negotiating factors, including but not limited to price, financing, terms, date of possession, and inclusion or exclusion of repairs, furnishings, or equipment. In addition, the purchase agreement should provide a period of time for you to complete appropriate inspections and investigations of the property before you are bound to complete the purchase. Your agent can advise you as to which investigations and inspections are recommended or required.

5. Buying a home is emotional. A home often symbolizes family, rest, and security — it's not just four walls and a roof. Because of this, home buying and selling can be an emotional undertaking. And for most people, a home is the biggest purchase they'll ever make. Having a concerned, but objective, third party helps you stay focused on both the emotional and financial issues most important to you.

*Source – National Association of Realtors

But just because a real estate agent is a REALTOR® doesn't automatically mean you can pick any REALTOR®. To pick yourself a top-notch professional, do the following:

General Research

The best place to start is by asking friends for referrals. If they have used an agent in the past they are happy about, you should definitely consider him/her if you are looking for a house in the same area. National Association of Realtors reported that Forty-four percent of buyers found their agent through a referral from a friend or family member. You can even do some initial research online. A recent study suggests that Nine out of ten home buyers used the Internet as one of the information sources in their home search process. First time home buyers were even more likely to use the Internet. Use websites like Yelp.com that provides reviews for agents. You can also Google to search for real estate agents in a particular area. Look for agents who seem to be well versed in the homes, schools, municipal services and other important information via their website or blogs.

How will you know which REALTOR® is right for you? Seek to work with an experienced Real Estate professional that works with buyers on a regular basis. A real pro will go the extra mile to show you that they will look out for your best interest and gain your respect. *Sincerity* is a key word here. This type of Real Estate Agent will act promptly to get you information about their team and their methods of doing business, along with quotes and references from past clients.

An experienced buyer's representative will ask many questions regarding your goals rather than tell you what they think you want to hear. You should also ask the following questions to find out more about the agent:

- How long you have been licensed for?
- Are you a Part-time or a Full-time agent?
- How accessible are you?
- Any other question important for your situation

Answers to these questions and your own comfort level with the real estate agent should help you in deciding the right realtor.

If you need recommendation for a good real estate agent, email me at *Shashank@ArcusLending.com* and I will direct you to the right agent. Make sure to mention where you plan to buy and what price range are you looking at.

Choosing a Loan Consultant

Choosing a Loan Consultant is like choosing a trusted financial advisor. Or maybe even more! With a financial advisor you may have the option of replacing him/her with someone else if you are not satisfied; you can't do that with a home purchase. So make sure, you do your due-diligence in choosing the loan consultant to handle probably the biggest financial decision yet of your life.

General Research

General research and short listing for a Loan Consultant is almost exactly like researching for Real Estate Agent. Start by asking your friends and families. Make sure you pick someone who is local and easily accessible.

Interviewing Process

Interview the referrals for your Loan Consultant. Comparing rates is just one part of the process. The main purpose is to learn and get the best advice. If they are just trying to sell you something and not actually analyzing your financial situation; chances are they are not offering you the best advice. But understand that to get the best advice, you will have to share your income, assets and credit score. After you have given them your situation and your financial goals let them advise you as to the best programs and products for your situation. Personally, I take well over one hour to do a mortgage planning exercise to advice the most suitable financing option.

Take a Pick

Upon interviewing those loan consultants, it's time to pick one. Sometimes, it may come down to a gut feeling. That is fine.

 **Who is better - Mortgage Broker or a Bank Loan Officer?**

The loan officers at a bank, credit union or other lending institution are employees who work to sell and process mortgages and other loans originated by their employer. They often have a wide variety of loans types to draw from, but all loans originate from one lending institution.

Mortgage brokers are professionals who are paid a fee to bring together lenders and borrowers. They usually work with dozens or even hundreds of lenders, not as employees, but as freelance agents.

A mortgage broker would usually have more options and wider selection of loan products. But a Bank loan officer may have better control on the loan process.

At the end of the day it's their individual expertise and your comfort level that should decide who do you go with. But stay away from online companies who only have a website and a toll-free number. Going through a mortgage process for the first time could be stressful sometimes; hence you would need someone local who is more accessible.

> If you need recommendation for a Loan Consultant, email me and I will direct you to the right person.

"Home is where the heart is"
Pliny the Elder

Beginning Your Home Search

In real estate they say – Location, Location, Location! Meaning the most important aspect in a house is Location. You can remodel the house and pretty much change everything; but you can't change the location. That is why usually even an average house in a good neighborhood costs more than a good house in an average neighborhood.

So where should you start your home search? Start by filling out the checklist on the next page. Once you have completed this, give this to your real estate agent so that both of you are on the same page.

Once you have looked at some houses, you will realize that no home is perfect. That's when you may want to revisit this checklist and make some changes to it.

Price Range: from $_____ to $_____

		Rank (1-5)
Property Features:		
# of Levels		
Age of the property		
Type of property*		
# of Bedrooms		
# of Bathrooms		
___ Car Garage		
Living Area (Sq Ft)		
Lot Size		
Back Yard Y/N		
Family Room Y/N		
Laundry Room Y/N		
Type of Appliances		
Central Air Conditioning		
Type of Flooring		
Storage		
Neighborhood Features:		
Commute to work		
Close to good schools		
Close to parks/playgrounds		

*Common types of properties:

Single Family Home: traditional lot with one home on it for one family.

Condominium: unit within a building where each owner holds title to the unit and some portion of the common property.

Townhouse: usually a multi-floored house which shares walls with one or two other townhouses.

Once you have liked a house that falls in your budget, you would like to make an offer on the house. The seller may get an offer to buy from multiple buyers including you. The seller with the guidance of the listing real estate agent decides which offer to accept. The decision is not always based on the highest offer. Probability of successful close of the transaction is usually given more weightage than the offer price. Make sure when you are making an offer, you are showcasing the strength of your credit qualification. Sometimes that may require submitting your credit scores and bank statement with your offer. A copy of pre-approval letter from a mortgage lender Is almost always required. In a market where demand of houses is more than supply, you might have to make several offers before one is accepted.

 **Are foreclosed & short-sale properties a good deal?**

DataQuick reported of the existing homes sold in California in October, 2009, 41.2 percent were properties that had been foreclosed on during the past year. That is the lowest since May last year when it was 39.8 percent. In October 2008 it was 52.4 percent. It reached a peak of 58.8 percent in February, 2009. Even though, the numbers show a downward trend, most of the current sale is being driven by foreclosed properties.

The chart below details 1 foreclosure in every X number of households as reported by Realtytrac.com

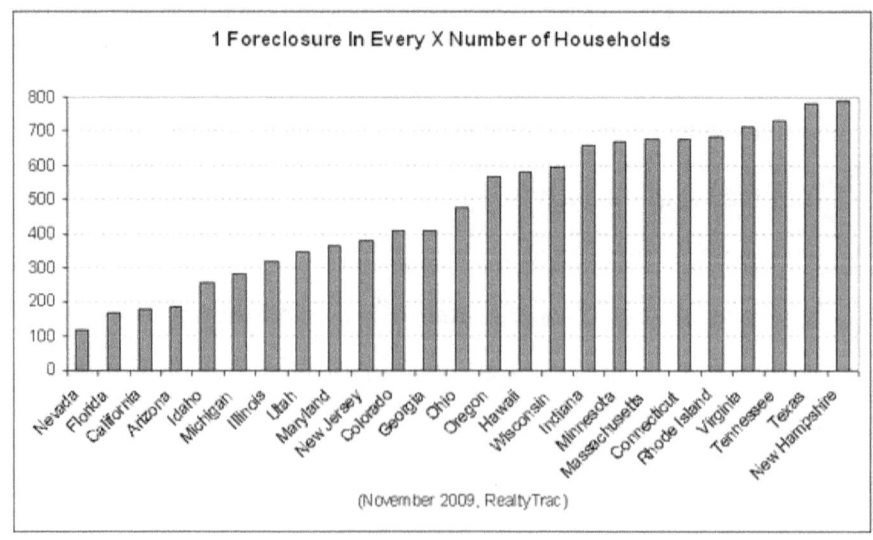

But before jumping on the bandwagon be cautioned that not all foreclosed houses are good deal. Most foreclosures sell at a discount, but the benefit of a lower sales price is often negated by the cost of repairs required to restore the home to a livable condition. Foreclosed properties often have not been maintained due to the distressed financial situation of the seller. Use the table below to learn about the 3 types of properties available in today's market:

	Regular Sale	*Short Sale*	*Foreclosed Property*
Owner	Seller	Seller	Bank
Seller	Seller	Seller & Bank(s)	Bank
Condition	Mostly Good – Average	Mostly Poor	Mostly Poor
Time to close	30-60 days	1-6 months	45-90 days
Ability to close	Easy	Very tough	Easy – Moderately tough
Good deal?	Maybe	Maybe	Usually Yes

"Home – that blessed word, which opens to the human heart the most perfect glimpse of heaven, and helps to carry it thither, as on an angel's wings."

Lydia M Child

The Nuances of your Purchase Contract

The process of purchasing a home is often much more complex than the average individual expects it to be. Items involved in your purchase contract can have a significant impact not only on the success of your purchase transaction, but on your stress level as well. I have listed out some of the important items you should be aware of, that require you to make decisions as a buyer entering into a purchase contract.

Loan or Financing Contingency

Loan contingency is the period of time the seller is giving you to obtain full, formal loan approval. It is important to include a financing contingency in your offer, as it makes the transaction dependent on you receiving the mortgage you've applied for. It specifies your cancellation rights if you are unable to obtain financing.

This contingency is typically between 10 and 21 days depending on what has been negotiated in the contract. The earnest money deposit you make at the time the offer is accepted will be put in jeopardy once the contingency for the loan has expired. In fact, pursuant to the terms of the contract, if the loan contingency has expired and you fail to close the purchase transaction, you could lose your earnest money deposit and not have the failure of obtaining loan approval to lean on as an excuse. Written pre-approval will help to eliminate problems in this area.

Contract Period

The contract period is the period of time in which all due diligence must be completed, including obtaining loan approval, property appraisal, home inspection reports, termite inspection, etc. Give yourself enough time for all due diligence to be completed for this very important purchase you are about to make. Typically, purchase contracts are drawn up for a period of 30, 45 or 60 days. However, it is really not uncommon for a purchase contract to be written with terms in excess of 60 days if the parties involved need that long of a period to complete all aspects of due diligence.

Home Inspection Contingency

As part of the negotiation in your purchase contract you and the seller will mutually agree upon the amount of time needed to complete all the home inspection procedures that are required. Utilizing an outside third party service to complete these inspections is highly recommended.

You will be provided with a report by the home inspection company that you should review very thoroughly to make sure there are no material defects in the property that you were not aware of, and which could subsequently have an impact on the value of the property. Once your home inspection contingency has expired, you no longer have the leverage to go back and renegotiate with the seller to resolve any issues revealed by the home inspection. If there are material defects, you and your real estate agent should renegotiate either a reduction in the purchase price to offset the cost of any necessary repairs or having the seller make the repairs prior to the close of the transaction. Buyers with limited cash reserves should most likely negotiate to have the repairs made prior to closing.

Termite Inspection

A termite inspection is required by the lender if it is listed in the purchase contract. The lender may also require an inspection if the appraisal states there is evidence of termite damage. On FHA loans inspection is required only under the following circumstances: when there is evidence of active infestation, if mandated by the state or local jurisdiction, if customary to the area, or at the lender's discretion.

If termites are present it is up to both parties to determine who will be responsible for the remedy of the problem. When you negotiate your contract make sure you state up front whether you want the property checked for termites.

Seller Rent Back

It is often the case that when the buyer and seller are unable to agree upon a specified closing date for the transaction, the real estate agents will negotiate a "rent back" period. This means the transaction closes, the loan funds and ownership of the property is transferred into the buyer's name, but the buyer does not take occupancy of the property until several days later. In this scenario, the buyer sets up a rental agreement, in which the property is leased back to the seller.

An important footnote to this somewhat common strategy is to make sure the seller is not occupying the property in a lease agreement for more than 30 days after the close of the purchase transaction. This would constitute a non-owner occupied purchase in the lender's eyes, and would cause the terms of the loan to change radically.

Seller Contributions

Depending on the seller's eagerness to close the transaction, the seller of a property will often become aggressive and offer to pay some or all of the closing costs, origination points and/or pre-paid items (interest, hazard insurance, tax escrows) associated with the purchase on the buyer's behalf. This common strategy can be very beneficial to the buyer, particularly if the buyer is short on funds to close. It can also be the vehicle that effectively drives the interest rate down and provides the buyer with a more affordable monthly payment.

The typical seller contribution is from 1% to 3% of the purchase price, based on the size of the down payment. Seller contributions may sometimes be isolated to non-recurring closing costs and/or origination points only. The lender will not permit the seller to contribute funds back to the buyer after the close of the transaction to accommodate repairs to the property. Items such as roof leakage or new carpet may not be covered by any seller contribution clause.

"Home is a name, a word, it is a strong one; stronger than magician ever spoke, or spirit ever answered to, in the strongest conjuration."

Charles Dickens

4 Cs of Lending

Capacity – Lenders usually look for a minimum of 2 years of work history in the same line of work. Any employment gaps or extended time off must to be explained. If you had a recent job change or if your income is derived from seasonal work, your income may be considered for qualifying purposes in certain situations. However, less than 2 years of work history may be acceptable if you have been studying and your current job is related to the subject you graduated in.

Cash – Cash is the funds that are required to close the purchase transaction. It's calculated as down payment + closing cost & pre paids. To qualify for some programs, you may even be required to have some cash left to cover for housing payment for few months.

Credit – Past credit performance serves as a guide in determining a borrower's attitude toward credit and predicting a borrower's future performance. If the credit history, despite adequate income, is poor, strong compensating factors will be necessary to approve the loan. Lenders usually examine the overall pattern of credit behavior, rather than isolated late payments. A period of financial difficulty in the past does not necessarily disqualify the borrower if they have re-established a good payment record for a considerable time period after the difficulty. To qualify not all collection accounts need to be paid off, but all Judgments have to be paid off to qualify.

Collateral – Collateral for a mortgage loan is the underlying property against which the loan is provided. While evaluating the collateral a lender's underwriter looks for security, safety and soundness of the property.

What if I had filed for Bankruptcy or Foreclosure?

If you had filed for foreclosure or deed-in-lieu of foreclosure in the previous three years, you would most likely be ineligible for a new loan.

If you had filed for a chapter 7 bankruptcy and the discharge date is less than 2 years you would be ineligible for a loan. For chapter 13 bankruptcies at least one year into the payout plan must have elapsed.

Some exceptions to the rule may be possible if there is evidence of significant extenuating circumstances and also an evidence of re-established good credit.

What if I am on contract employment?

If you are on a contract and don't get paid a pay stub on a regular basis or get paid a 1099 you would be considered self employed. In this case your income could be averaged over last 2 years to arrive at the qualifying income. That could mean your qualifying income could be less than your current income. Also, if you have claimed deductions for your expenses in your tax returns, that could be adjusted against your income.

Marriage and Mortgages FAQs

Q: Can one spouse's low score negatively affect the couple's chances of securing a mortgage?

A: If a couple is applying for credit jointly, then yes. One person's lower score can negatively impact the interest rate the couple will be offered. This is because every borrower has three credit scores, and lenders use the lowest "middle" credit score of the two borrowers. We have seen many situations in the past in which one borrower was dropped from the application – but only if the lower score belongs to a non-working spouse. This can create a serious issue, however, if the income is needed in order to qualify.

Q: *Could one spouse's bad credit negatively affect the other?*

A: Yes, if one borrower has negative credit items, such as late payments or a foreclosure, the worst of the two will be taken into account when considering your mortgage application. With a foreclosure, this could mean having to wait up to 3-4 years to be eligible for a loan again.

Q: Does the lender use both people as a measure of creditworthiness, or is it possible to focus on the spouse with the better score?

A: In the past, this was possible, but now the lowest score of the two (or however many) people are on the application is used. This could also include parents that are co-signing a loan for one of their children.

"There is no sanctuary of virtue like home."

Edward Everett

Financing Options

Loan Types:

Fixed Rate Mortgages: These mortgages have the same interest rate through the term of the loan. So if a loan starts with say 5.5%, the rate would remain the same till the end of the term. Most common terms for fixed rate mortgages are 30 and 15 year fixed. But 20 and 10 year fixed options are also available.

Adjustable Rate Mortgages: These are also called ARMs or Variable rate mortgages. On these loans, the interest rate is fixed for a certain number of months/years and becomes variable after that. The most common are 3, 5 and 7 year ARMs in which the rate is fixed for 3, 5 and 7 year. The term of the loan almost always is 30 years.

 **How Adjustable Rate Mortgages work?**

Adjustable Rate Mortgages have three main features: Margin, Index, and Caps. The Margin is the fixed portion of the adjustable rate. It remains the same for the duration of the loan.

The Index is the variable portion. This is what makes an ARM adjustable. Margin + Index = Interest Rate.

It's important to understand that there are many different indices: The 11th District Cost of Funds (COFI), the Monthly Treasury Average (MTA), The One Year Treasury Bill, the Six Month Libor, etc. Each index has its own strengths and weaknesses; some are slow moving, others are more aggressive.

The third and final component of Adjustable Rate Mortgages is Caps. Caps limit how much the rate can fluctuate over time. Annual Caps limit changes to the annual rate, whereas Life Caps provide a worst case scenario over the life of the loan.

Hybrid Rate Mortgages: These mortgages start as an ARM loan, but have the option of converting into a fixed loan at a later date.

 **When to pick ARM vs. Fixed Rate?**

When you are trying to make a decision on whether to take an Adjustable Rate Mortgage or a Fixed, you should consider two factors:

- How long you plan to stay in the property?
- What is the difference in the interest rate between an ARM & a Fixed?

Let me elaborate this:

Rates on ARMs are usually lower than fixed rate loans. But the rates are fixed usually only for 5 or 7 years. So if you do plan to live in your house for more than that period, you may risk your mortgage adjusting into a very high rate prevalent at that time. However, if the current interest rate difference is substantial you may still want to take the risk. For example assume for a $400,000 loan the fixed rate is 5.25%, while for a 5 year ARM the rate is 4.5%. The payment on a fixed rate would be $2209, while for the ARM that would be $2027, saving you $182 a month. In 5 years you would have saved $10,920 in monthly payments. If the rate on the ARM adjusts to 6% after that and assume you pay at that rate for next 25 years. Then you would pay $2349 per month for next 25 years. So on the ARM loan you would pay $121,620 for first 5 years and then $704,700 for next 25 years, a total of $826,320. On the 30 year fixed rate loan over 30 years you would pay $2209 x 360 = $795,240.

As you can see in the example if you were to keep the house for 5-7 years it absolutely made sense to get an ARM. However if you kept the loan for 30 years the fixed rate option made more sense. In your case the numbers may be different and also for an ARM loan it's impossible to predict the future interest rate. So make sure you factor both aspects mentioned above before deciding on what kind of loan program works better for you.

Interest Only Mortgages: In a mortgage like this, the monthly payment goes towards the payment of only interest. So the principal balance remains the same. Usually after a certain number of years an Interest only loan converts to a fully amortizing loan, meaning payment is required to be made towards both principal & interest.

 What Is a Prepayment Penalty?

A prepayment penalty is a fee charged to borrowers that make full payment on their mortgage, or pay off a substantial portion (generally anything exceeding 20% of the total loan amount), ahead of schedule. This is a clause written into some contracts to protect the lender's book of business in exchange for providing a lower interest rate, or for providing financing to a high-risk borrower.

Prepayment penalties vary with different lenders, but generally apply to a one, two, three, or five-year period of time. This fee can be expressed as either a specific number of months' interest or a percentage of the outstanding balance. A 'hard' prepayment penalty applies to either the refinance or the sale of a property. A contract written with a 'soft' prepayment penalty permits the borrower to sell their property without incurring a penalty, but does restrict refinancing for a set period of time. It is important for you to know that a prepayment penalty is the borrower's *choice* and should never be considered a requirement!

Loan Programs

Conforming Loans – These are loans that meet the guidelines of Government Sponsored Enterprises (GSEs) namely Fannie Mae & Freddie Mac. The basic conforming loan limit is $417,000. These loans require a minimum down payment of 5%-10%.

Conforming Jumbo Loans – One of the provisions of the Stimulus bill signed by the President in February 2009 was to increase the maximum conforming jumbo loan amount to $729,750 through end of 2009. That has now been extended through 2010. The down payment on these loans is 10%-15% and the interest rates are higher than the basic conforming loan amounts.

Jumbo Loans – Loan amounts over $729,750 are considered pure jumbo loans. These loans may require up to 20% or more down payment and would typically have higher interest rates than any kind of conforming loans.

VA Loan - Mortgage loans available to eligible US veterans. A veteran must have served 180 days of active service. VA guaranteed loans are made by private lenders, such as banks or mortgage companies, for the purchase of a home for a buyer's own personal occupancy. These loans offer competitive rates and require little or no down payment.

USDA Home Loans – A USDA home loan is a government guaranteed home loan which lends up to 100% of the purchase price and may even include some closing costs. These are only offered in rural areas and have loan limits based on geographic location or income limits based on family size.

One of the biggest difficulties many first-time home buyers face is a lack of down payment and the necessary funds for closing costs. However, even with the widespread availability of "no-money-down programs" evaporating in the credit crisis, one national no-down payment program still remains: USDA Rural Development home loans. Guaranteed by the USDA (United States Department of Agriculture), this program might make you think that you have to buy farmland or live "in the country" to qualify, but this is often not the case. In fact, you might be surprised to see just how many neighborhoods actually do qualify as rural development areas. For this program, the term "rural" really applies to those areas with a lower population or fewer homes, not necessarily those areas and neighborhoods far outside of the city.

There are several benefits of the USDA loan program besides no money down. The program also does not require private mortgage insurance, and the seller is allowed to pay all of your closing costs and pre-paid items up to 6.00% of the total sales price of the property. And while this is great news for first-time home buyers, it's important to note that you don't have to be a first-timer to qualify for a USDA loan.

Other than the location of the property you're seeking to buy, there is one other limitation to this valuable program that you must consider: your income. Luckily, however, these numbers have recently increased to allow more potential buyers to take advantage of this special program. For households in non-high cost areas, with up to four people, the income limit is $70,750. In households where 5-8 people reside, the income limitation is $93,400. These income limitations are guidelines and, in some cases, may be exceeded.

To know more about these loans visit USDA rural development home page at http://www.rurdev.usda.gov/

Piggy Back Loan – "Piggy Back Loan" is a slang term, which really is another way of describing 1st and 2nd mortgages that close concurrently. In today's mortgage lending environment, obtaining a piggy back loan can be very difficult if a borrower has less than 20% for a down payment. In such instances, obtaining one mortgage with Private Mortgage Insurance may be the only option.

Private Mortgage Insurance - In the event that you do not have a 20% down payment, the lender may allow a smaller down payment, sometimes as low as 3.5%. However, with a smaller down payment, borrowers are usually required to carry private mortgage insurance on the loan. Private mortgage insurance comes in two forms: upfront - paid at closing, and/or monthly. A lender may require some combination of both upfront and monthly mortgage insurance. The amount required is determined based on program type, property type, credit score and loan-to-value ratio.

FAQ Why Pay Private Mortgage Insurance (PMI)?

Private Mortgage Insurance (PMI) is required by most lenders when a borrower puts less than 20% down on a purchase loan. Paid for by the borrower, PMI not only protects the lender from foreclosure, it also enables many buyers to qualify for loans and purchase real estate when they couldn't have otherwise. On January 1st, 2007, legislation went into effect making PMI tax deductible for new borrowers whose personal adjusted gross Income is $100,000 or less. This has created additional opportunities for many buyers to finance a more expensive home or, in some cases, to obtain a lower monthly payment, while reducing annual income taxes.

An alternative financing option that borrowers may also consider involves taking out two home loans concurrently. The second loan commonly referred to as a "piggyback loan", can take the form of a traditional home loan or a Home Equity Line of Credit (HELOC). It supplements the borrower's funds to help them achieve a 20% down payment, eliminating the need for PMI. However, in most cases PMI can be cancelled once the accumulated equity has reached 20% of the home's value, while a second home loan will have to be paid back in full regardless. Factor in the new PMI tax benefit, and a borrower's monthly payment may actually be lower with PMI versus a piggyback loan scenario.

Choosing PMI is not a one-size-fits-all decision. It's a loan consultant's job to weigh borrowers' long-term goals and to provide comprehensive solutions that clearly explain all of the pros and cons of each mortgage option available.

First Time Home Buyer Program - Mortgage loans with special qualifying terms for those who have not owned real estate in the previous 3 years. Although the programs and terms vary by state, they often offer down payment and closing cost assistance. These loans typically have household income limits.

> Email me and I will send you a list of special First Time Buyer Loan Programs and Down Payment Assistance in your area.

Pre Qualification Vs Pre-Approval

Pre-qualification is the starting point in your search for mortgage financing. A quick snapshot is taken which includes income, existing debt, savings, length of employment, etc. All of these factors will then be analyzed to determine your loan eligibility.

Pre-approval is written documentation that shows you have the support of a lender who is willing to finance you. It means your loan application has been reviewed by an underwriter. Based on your income, debt ratio and savings, the underwriter provides the dollar amount you are eligible to borrow. Now you can shop around for houses that fit into that loan amount category.

Seeking pre-approval for financing prior to making an offer on a property is a sound strategy that can help you get the best deal possible, especially if you plan to make a minimal down payment. The seller is often leery of the stability and reliability of the buyer if the buyer is only capable of making a down payment of 10% or less. This can cause the buyer to lose a significant amount of negotiating ability, by being perceived as a weak buyer rather than a strong one. This is why it is very important to get full loan credit approval in advance and provide a written confirmation of the loan approval when an offer is made. This shows it is a done deal and you are perceived to be a cash buyer.

Bottomline - Full credit approval can easily save you few thousand dollars on the purchase price of your home.

Rate Shopping

Shopping for the best interest rate possible has always been the consumer's primary objective when borrowing money. As well it should be! The challenge with this strategy is that there is much misleading information released on the subject by various media. Internet web sites and email marketing, along with other media such as radio, television and billboard advertising, have brought the

importance of interest rates to the forefront of consumers' minds.

The problem for the consumer with this type of marketing is that it is designed to make the lender's phone ring. Often, the advertiser offers a ridiculously low interest rate, with the intent of using a "bait-and-switch" technique once the client is reeled in. This is often done through short pricing. Short pricing is a term that is used when a lender offers an extremely attractive interest rate, but that rate is only locked-in for a very brief period of time.

The average consumer enters into a purchase contract to buy a home for at least 30 days. Pricing on an interest rate locked in for a 7-day period is of no use to most prospective home buyers. It simply isn't enough time to complete the transaction. While the billboard advertising or Internet banner ad may boast a terrific rate, the lock-in period is often not realistic in terms of providing enough time to negotiate a purchase contract and close the deal. Be very careful when shopping for interest rates. Make sure that when you are quoted a rate, you are asking the lender what the lock duration is. Make sure that lock period allows you enough time to complete your purchase transaction.

Another common marketing ploy that makes interest rates appear attractive is geared around the manner in which fees are presented. All lenders are required by law to state the real cost of the financing through the Annual Percentage Rate (APR) each time an interest rate is quoted in advertising. APR takes many of the fees associated with the loan into consideration, and it is usually listed in fine print as a disclaimer.

Advertisers often list a low interest rate in large bold type, but the higher APR indicates in fine print that several points are being charged to get that rate.

While APR can be helpful in comparing rates seen in advertising, it is important for consumers to know that lenders use different methods to calculate APR. Hence it is not an entirely failsafe method for comparing interest rates.

Additionally, the consumer must take into consideration that the interest rate is not the only important factor in obtaining financing. Another equally important question to answer is, "How long do you need to borrow this money?"

The length of time you need to borrow the money has a profound impact on whether or not you should be paying upfront fees (points), and likewise has bearing on your loan program selection.

Statistically, homeowners move every 7 to 10 years. One of the common mistakes made by home buyers is automatically selecting a 30-year fixed rate loan program for financing instead of evaluating other options. If the buyer is somewhat transient in their job or is planning a family in the near future, the home may not really meet their long-term needs.

In such a scenario, an interest rate that is fixed for five, seven or ten years may be a much more realistic option. This allows the buyer to capitalize on a low introductory rate and save a significant amount of money, which can then go toward the down payment on their next home. It is of utmost importance to work with an experienced loan consultant that understands some of the practical aspects of financial planning. A well-versed consultant will ask you many questions about your short- and long-term goals, and assist you in choosing a loan program that is truly suited to those goals.

Mortgage Interest Rate Myth

This may come as a shock to many borrowers, but it's absolutely true. Mortgage interest rates are *not* set by the Federal Reserve and, contrary to popular belief; mortgage rates are *not* directly tied to the yields of US Treasury bills, bonds, or notes –including the 10-year Treasury Note. That's right. Despite what you might hear in the media, mortgage interest rates are actually set by lending institutions, and are based solely on the performance of mortgage-backed securities.

For years now, the media and inexperienced loan officers everywhere have suggested that the 10-year Treasury Note, a government-backed security, is directly tied to mortgage interest rates, that the two are separated by a specific interval – which is simply not true.

 **Typical closing cost in a purchase transaction:**

When you apply for a loan you will get a Good Faith Estimate that will give you an estimate of all closing costs and pre-paids.

Also note that below mentioned fees are typical for a transaction, but could vary depending on the service provider and your needs as a buyer. You can also negotiate with the seller to pay for some or all of the closing cost.

Credit Report Fee – Fee to cover for the cost of credit report $15 - $25.

Appraisal Fee – An Appraiser is hired to give an estimate of the value of the property. A fee is paid to him/her for the services $350-$500.

Loan Origination fee – Popularly known as points. 1 point is equal to 1% of the loan amount. It could be anywhere between 0%-3%.

Processing Fee – Fee paid to cover the processing cost of a loan $495-$695.

Underwriting fee – Fee charged by the lender to cover the underwriting and administrative expenses $650-$1200.

Upfront mortgage insurance premium – On FHA Loans 1.75% of the loan amount is charged as the upfront mortgage insurance premium (UFMIP). The buyer has the option of either paying it as an out of pocket expense or adding this to the principal balance.

Pre Paid Interest – Depending on the time of month your loan closes, you pay a per diem interest from that day to the end of the month.

Taxes and Homeowner's Insurance – You may be required to reimburse the seller, prorated depending on the month you close. You will also need to pay for the entire year of Homeowner's insurance premium upfront.

Impound Account – On some loans with impounds (mandatory for FHA loans) you may be required to put a certain amount for Insurance & taxes into a special reserve account held by the lender.

Title and escrow fees - These fees differ by who pays for what in different counties.

 **What is Title Insurance?**

Title insurance is a policy that is usually issued by a title company to protect the lender against something that might have happened in the past, rather than something that might occur in the future. In essence, an extensive search of public records is conducted by the title company to validate who has held title to the property in the past. The lender wants to know if there are any liens, judgments or easements on the property that they should be aware of.

But title insurance also guards against hidden risks or unknown factors that might cause an encumbrance at some point in the future, such as unknown heirs, forged deeds or wills, misinterpreted wills, false impersonation of the true owner of the property, deeds signed over by persons of unsound mind, or defects in the recording of past titles. Title insurance covers the cost of the title search, and any legal fees that may result from any dispute over past property ownership. It is required by the lender and paid for by the buyer.

The smart home buyer will also purchase title insurance to protect their own interests. This is a one-time premium that protects the buyer or their heirs, as long as they retain an interest in the property.

Should I Pay points or not?

Points are up-front fees paid to obtain a better interest rate on a loan. One point equals one percent of the loan amount. A lower interest rate may result in a lower monthly payment, but it is important to consider how long you intend to be in the loan, and to compare current rates to historical market trends.

If you take out a $300,000 mortgage and decide to pay one point, this translates into an up-front closing cost of $3,000. Paying a point up front saves $100 a month but it will take 30 months to recuperate the cost of that point. If you decide to refinance or sell the home before the 30-month mark, your money is lost. In this case, you would benefit financially by remaining in the home longer than the 30 months.

Rates run in cycles. When rates are at historical lows, it is sensible to pay points if you plan to live in the home for an extended period of time. It is unlikely that rates will go down; hence, there will be no need to refinance. When rates are up, there is a strong likelihood that they will come down. This is no time to pay points. The chances of refinancing in the future are extremely high, and you will likely not be in the loan long enough to recuperate the cost of the points.

 **How to reduce cash to close?**

Cash to close is the money that you need to bring at the closing table. This is a sum of:

- Downpayment
- Closing Cost
- Pre-Paids

If you can reduce one or more of these 3 items, you can essentially bring down the cash you need to close on your home purchase. Down payment can be reduced by choosing a loan program that has a low down payment requirement like an FHA Loan or an USDA loan (more details are provided in the Financing Options chapter).

Paying a slightly higher interest rate may result in the lender not charging you any origination points. In some cases, they may even credit you for some closing cost. You can also request the seller to pay for some part of your closing cost.

Not much can be done with Pre-Paids and also the effect on the total cash to close is minimal. However if you close towards the end of the month, you pay lesser pre-paid interest. Also closing the transaction in certain months could translate into lesser reserves for Property Taxes. For California - May, June and December closing typically have lower reserves requirements.

"Home, the spot of earth supremely blessed. A dearer, sweeter spot than all the rest."

Robert Montgomery

FHA and other First-Time Buyer Loan Programs

 **HOMEOWNERSHIP** The Federal Housing Administration (FHA) program first began in 1934 in an effort to encourage home ownership despite the difficult economic times of the era. The program enables consumers who may not qualify for a standard loan to obtain the financing they need to purchase a home without income limitations.

FHA loans differ from typical loans in that they are insured by the Federal Housing Administration, which is a part of the Department of Housing and Urban Development (HUD). Because this insurance reduces the lender's risk on the loan, lenders have greater flexibility with regard to approving loans.

The maximum loan amount usually changes every year. For 2010 the maximum limit is $729,750. You can go here to find out what is the loan amount limit for your county - https://entp.hud.gov/idapp/html/hicostlook.cfm. The down payment can be as low as 3.5% of the property value. These loans are increasingly becoming more popular with First Time Home Buyers. Below are some of the highlights of the program:

- There is no cap on annual household income to qualify for an FHA loan.
- The down payment can be in the form of a gift.
- A credit score of as low as 620 is acceptable.
- Seller can contribute up to 3% of property price towards closing cost.
- Non-occupying borrowers like your parents can co-sign on the loan and help you qualify.
- Past Bankruptcies and Foreclosures are acceptable too with some seasoning.

A special type of FHA loan called 203 (k) loan, helps you buy properties that require thousands of dollars to remedy deficiencies in the property. FHA loans also provide added flexibility when it comes to closing costs and the down payment. Many of the closing costs can be added into the loan, and a down payment of less than 3.5% of the purchase price is required. The down payment may be obtained as a gift from a family member or through a down-payment assistance program. FHA loans are processed just like any other loan, and they provide a wonderful opportunity for consumers who are seeking to achieve home ownership!

It pays to go Green: FHA has an Energy Efficient Mortgage (EEM). EEMs recognize that reduced utility expenses can permit a homeowner to pay a higher mortgage to cover the cost of the energy improvements on top of the approved mortgage. FHA EEMs provide mortgage insurance for a person to purchase a principal residence and incorporate the cost of energy efficient improvements into the mortgage. To be eligible for inclusion in the mortgage, the energy efficient improvements must be cost effective, meaning that the total cost of the improvements is less than the total present value of the energy saved over the useful life of the energy improvement.

Six Myths of FHA Lending

Though FHA Lending now represents more than 30% of mortgages, there are still a lot of misconceptions that both real estate agents and the buyers have about this program. All the myths that I have listed below have been raised to me numerous times.

1. *It takes longer to close an FHA Loan-* Towards the 2nd half of 2008 when FHA loans started exploding; most of the lenders were caught off guard. They did not have enough trained underwriters to take decisions on the loans that were being sent their way. That resulted in longer turn times for FHA loans. Within months, lenders realized that this was soon becoming the fastest mortgage product on the block. Since then they have staffed themselves adequately on the FHA underwriting side and

hence it's not atypical anymore for FHA loans to close in 30 days or less.

2. *Interest Rates are higher* - While interests rates are situation specific and can potentially change multiple times just in a day, FHA loans are usually priced the same as conventional. Sometimes they could be cheaper while at other times they could be slightly expensive.

3. *Closing Cost is higher* - FHA charges 1.75% up front Mortgage Insurance as   closing cost. That could make you think that you will have to bring that extra 1.75% to closing table. While that 1.75% is considered a closing cost, it's added to the loan amount, e.g. if your base loan amount was $400,000, your final loan amount actually becomes $407,000. As you can see FHA loans do not increase the amount of closing cost that you need to bring at closing.

4. *Income Caps to Qualify* - To qualify for FHA loans there are absolutely no house hold income caps. Meaning you could be making $1 million a year (or more) and could still be eligible for an FHA loan.

5. *Can't sell/refinance quickly*- FHA loans just like most of the conventional loans have no Pre-payment Penalty. What that means is you can sell your house or refinance anytime you wish after closing the transaction.

6. *Appraisal Requirements are tougher* -In December 2005, FHA made a number of changes to appraisal guidelines allowing for

"As-Is" appraisals even if minor defects to the property conditions exist. FHA appraisals now only require repairs for conditions that rise above cosmetic defects, minor defects, or normal wear and tear. Mostly, the appraisal requirements now resemble that of Conventional mortgages.

The table below compares FHA Loan with Conventional. As you will see both types of loans have their own benefits and it all depends on your specific situation which one is better suited for you.

LOAN FEATURES	CONVENTIONAL	FHA
Max Loan Amount	$729,750	$729,750
Max LTV	95%	96.5%
UFMIP	0	1.75%
PMI	Up to .89%	Up to .55%
PMI	Only for LTVs>80%	At all LTVs
Non occupant co-borrower	Not Allowed	Allowed
Declining Market Policy	Yes	No
Higher Rates for Condos	Yes, >75% LTV	Same as Single Family
Min credit score at max LTV	680/720 (Based on the loan amount)	620/640 (Based on the lender)

Occupancy	All Types	Only Primary Residence
All funds can be gifted	No	Yes
Impounds	Optional <90% LTV	Always mandatory
Manufactured Housing	Limited Options	Allowed
Pre-Payment Penalty	No	No

Other Loan Programs suitable for First Time Home Buyers

 Homepath was created to facilitate the purchase of the bulk of REO properties currently serviced/guaranteed by FNMA (Fannie Mae).

Highlights:

- As little as 3% down allowed for owner occupied!
- As little as 10% down for non owner occupied and 2nd Homes!
- No Mortgage Insurance!
- No Appraisal Needed - Value determined by Sales Price
- You may qualify even if your credit is less than perfect
- Loan Amounts up to $801,950 allowed
- Loan Term Available : 30 Year Fixed
- Transaction Purpose : Purchase Only

Borrower Eligibility

- First Time Homebuyers allowed
- Non-Perm Resident Aliens not allowed
- Non-Occupant Co-borrowers not allowed

Here's How to get started: Check www.homepath.com to ensure property is eligible for HomePath financing.

Cal HFA California Housing Finance Agency or CalHFA in short recently launched it's new program called Cal 30 - Conventional for First Time Home Buyers in the state of California. This conventional first mortgage features a fixed interest rate, fully amortized loan over a 30-year term. It has a maximum Loan-to-Value (LTV) of 95%. Below are some of the other highlights of the program:

Maximum Loan Amount - The loan amount is limited to the maximum Fannie Mae conforming loan limits. Currently, this is $417,000. Fannie Mae high balance loan limits are not available.

Property Eligibility - Sales price of the home cannot exceed CalHFA's sales price limits established for the county in which the property is located. Property can be a single-family, one-unit residence, including approved condominium /PUDs. Manufactured housing is not permitted.

Private Mortgage Insurance - Private Mortgage Insurance (MI) is required on all Cal30 Conventional loans with LTV greater than 80.00%.

What are the eligibility requirements for you to qualify for this loan?

- Be a U.S. citizen, permanent resident alien or qualified alien
- Be a first-time homebuyer, except for qualified veterans pursuant to the Heroes Earnings Assistance and Relief Tax Act of 2008 or unless home is located in a federally designated Targeted Area
- Occupy the property as your primary residence.
- Borrower's income cannot exceed the published Cal30 income limits established for the county in which the property is located
- Loans in federally designated targeted areas must comply with the same income limits.
- Borrower(s) may not own another residential property at time of closing
- Meet credit, income and loan requirements of CalHFA, Fannie Mae, the lender and the mortgage insurer

First Look by Fannie Mae

 Fannie Mae recently announced a program called "First Look" which will help First Time Home Buyers compete with investors for foreclosed homes.

Under the program, dubbed First Look, Fannie plans to consider offers only from potential owner-occupants and certain public-housing entities during the first 15 days in which a foreclosed home is on the market.

Many investors can move faster on home purchases because they are able to pay cash and don't have to wait to qualify for a loan and get an appraisal. If you are a First Time Home Buyer, a lot of you could be going through the hassle of making offers on several properties and often losing bidding wars to investors.

In addition to the 15-day head start, home buyers using Neighborhood Stabilization Program funds, HOME Investment Partnerships Program funds, local housing trust funds, or charitable foundation funds may also qualify for reduced deposit requirements of as low as $500, reserved contract periods in which buyers can renegotiate their offers, and up to 45 days to close, up from the usual 30 days.

 **How to reduce monthly payment?**

Monthly housing payment consists of following:

- Mortgage Payment (Principal & Interest)
- Property Taxes
- Homeowner's Insurance
- Mortgage Insurance (If applicable)
- HOA Dues (If applicable)

Property taxes and HOA dues cannot be changed. Mortgage Insurance may be reduced by making larger down payment. You can shop for a Homeowner's insurance policy to get a better premium rate. But the biggest component of housing payment is of course Mortgage Payment. There is only one of 3 ways to reduce it:

- Lower interest rate
- Longer loan term (At this time 30 years is the longest term available)
- Interest only option – You could opt for a loan that allows you to make only an interest payment. Note that there are very few loan programs that allow you to make interest only payment.

"Home is the most popular and will be the most enduring of all earthly establishments."

Channing Pollock

Credit 101

The subject of credit scoring has become an increasingly hot topic, and for good reason. For many years, the general public only associated the concept of credit scoring with the need to purchase high-ticket items such as a new car or a home. Today, credit scoring goes much further.

Your credit score can affect your ability to get a good rate on commodities such as car insurance, cell phones, or even determine whether or not you get the job that you want. Indeed, the financial snapshot provided by the credit score has also become a gauge for many employers, especially those who seek to place employees in a position of financial responsibility.

Why Your Credit Score is so important

The credit scoring model seeks to quantify the likelihood of a consumer to pay off debt without being more than 90 days late at any time in the future. Credit scores can range between a low score of 300 and a high score of 850. The higher the score, the better it is for the consumer, because a high credit score translates into a low interest rate. This can save literally thousands of dollars in financing fees over the life of the loan.

Only one out of 1,300 people in the United States have a credit score above 800. These are people with a stellar credit rating that get the best interest rates. On the other hand, one out of every eight prospective home buyers is faced with the possibility that they may not qualify for the home loan they want because they have a score falling between 500 and 600.

The Five Factors of Credit Scoring

Credit scores are comprised of five factors. Points are awarded for each component, and a high score is most favorable. The factors are listed below in order of importance.

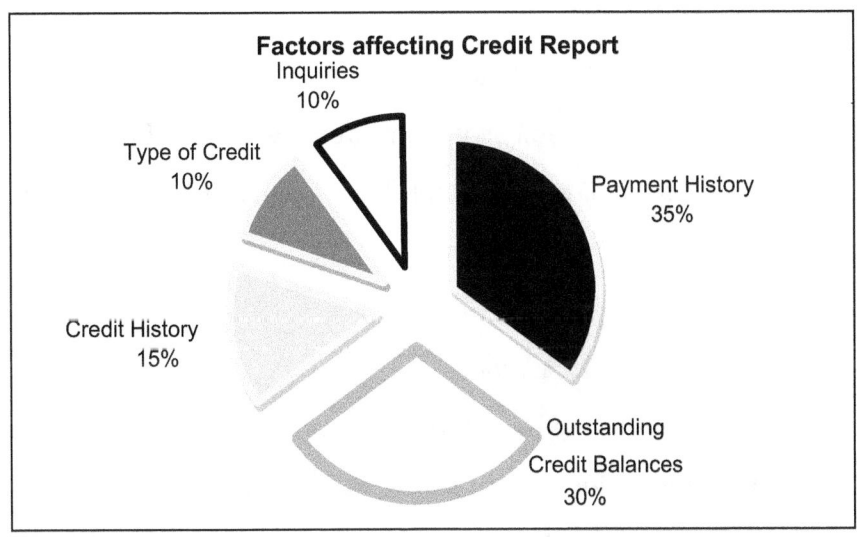

1. Payment History – 35% Impact

Paying debt on time and in full has the greatest positive impact on your credit score. Late payments, judgments and charge-offs all have a negative impact. Missing a high payment will have a more severe impact than missing a low payment, and delinquencies that have occurred in the last two years carry more weight than older items.

2. Outstanding Credit Balances – 30% Impact

This factor marks the ratio between the outstanding balance and available credit. Ideally, the consumer should make an effort to keep balances as close to zero as possible, and definitely below 30% of the available credit limit when trying to purchase a home.

3. Credit History – 15% Impact

This portion of the credit score indicates the length of time since a particular credit line was established. A seasoned borrower will always be stronger in this area.

4. Type of Credit – 10% Impact

A mix of auto loans, credit cards and mortgages is more positive than a concentration of debt from credit cards only.

5. Inquiries – 10% Impact

This percentage of the credit score quantifies the number of inquiries made on a consumer's credit within a six-month period. Each "hard inquiry" can cost from two to 25 points on a credit score, but the maximum number of inquiries that will reduce the score is ten. In other words, 11 or more inquiries within a six-month period will have no further impact on the borrower's credit score. Note that if you run a credit report on yourself, it will have no effect on your score.

Remember that the credit score is a computerized calculation. Personal factors like income or assets are not taken into consideration when a credit report is generated. It is merely a snapshot of today's credit profile for any given borrower, and it can fluctuate dramatically within the course of a week.

 **How does a low credit score affect my interest rate?**

Lenders estimate your ability to pay back money based on your credit score. The risk factor they take on is built-in to your interest rate as a financing fee. Therefore, a low credit score results in a higher interest rate, higher monthly fees, and a higher amount of interest being paid over the total life of the loan.

A borrower with a credit score of less than 620 would be questionable to an underwriter. While the lender may agree to provide financing, the increased interest rate is factored into the monthly payment.

 **What if I Have No Credit?**

Establishing a good credit history has never been as important as it is today.

It's not just that you'll need good credit to get decent rates when you're ready to buy a home or a car. Your credit history can determine whether you get a good job, a decent apartment or reasonable rates on insurance. It's a classic Catch-22: You've got to have credit to get credit. So where do you start?

If you're just starting out, you have a once-in-a-lifetime opportunity to build a credit history the right way. Here's what to do, and what to avoid.

Piggyback on someone else's good credit

The fastest way to establish a credit history can be to "borrow" another's record, either by being added to a credit card as an "authorized" or joint user or by getting someone to co-sign a loan for you.

Being added as an "authorized user" has its risks, for you as well as the person giving you access to the card.

If your father makes you an authorized user of his credit card, for example, his history with that account can be imported to your credit bureau file, giving you an instant credit record. If he has handled the account well, that reflects well on you. But if he hasn't, his mistakes would also become yours.

Even if you trust the person adding you to the card, you may not be able to piggyback on his or her credit. Some credit issuers won't report authorized users to the credit bureaus, particularly if the user is not married to the original card holder. If the point is to give you a credit history, the person who's adding you as an authorized user should call the issuer and ask how (or if) your status as a user will be reported.

Apply for a secured credit card

If you can't get a regular credit card, apply for the secured version. These require you to deposit money with a lender; your credit limit is usually equal to the deposit.

Your credit union, if you have one, is a good place to start looking for a secured card. You can also check with the bank where you have your checking account. However, if the issuer doesn't report to the credit bureaus, the card won't help build your credit history.

Get an installment loan

To get the best credit score, you need a mix of different credit types including revolving accounts (credit cards, lines of credit) and installment accounts (auto loans, personal loans, mortgages).

Use revolving accounts lightly but regularly

For a credit score to be generated, you have to have had credit for at least six months, with at least one of your accounts updated in the past six months.

Using your cards regularly should ensure that your report is updated regularly. It also will keep the lender interested in you as a customer. If you get a credit card and never use it, the issuer could cancel the account.

Ultimately, experts say that it is best to have three to five credit cards, and no more than that. You should keep your balances as low as possible. If you have a credit account with a zero balance, do not close the account.

Instead, make a small purchase so the card shows up as an active account on your credit report, and you will be awarded points for your long-term credit history.

Do's and Don'ts during the Loan Process

These are just a few tips to consider as you seek to obtain mortgage financing.

When you fill out a credit application, they run a credit report for the underwriter. Each lender and each loan program has different guidelines they must follow. You should not do anything that will have an adverse effect on your credit score while your loan is in process. We know it's tempting... If you're moving into a new home, you might be thinking about purchasing new appliances or furniture, but this is really not the right time to go shopping with your credit cards. You'll want to remain in a stable position until the loan closes and give your lender the opportunity to help you lock in the best interest rate they can possibly get for you.

Here is a handy list of do's and don'ts that you should adhere to after your loan application has been submitted to the lender.*

Don't apply for new credit of any kind – If you receive invitations to apply for new lines of credit, don't respond. If you do, that company will pull your credit report and this will have an adverse effect on your credit score. Likewise, don't establish new lines of credit for furniture, appliances, computers, etc.

Don't pay off Collections or Charge-Offs – Once your loan application has been submitted, don't pay off collections unless the lender specifically asks you to in order to secure the loan. Generally, paying off old collections causes a drop in the credit score. The lender is only looking at last two years of activity.

Don't close Credit Card accounts – If you close a credit card account, it can affect your ratio of debt to available credit which has a 30% impact on your credit score. If you really want to close an account, do it after you close your mortgage loan.

Don't max out or over charge existing Credit Cards – Running up your credit cards is the fastest way to bring your score down, and it could drop up to 100 points overnight. Once you are engaged in the loan process, try to keep your credit cards below 30% of the available credit limit.

Don't consolidate debt to one or two cards – Once again, you don't want to change your ratio of debt to available credit. Likewise, you want to keep beneficial credit history on the books.

Don't raise red flags to the Underwriter – Don't co-sign on another person's loan, or change your name and address. The less activity that occurs while your loan is in process, the better it is for you.

Do join a Credit Watch program – Your bank, credit union or credit card company may be able to provide you with a free credit watch program that can alert you to any changes in your credit report. This can be a safeguard to help you intervene before the underwriter sees a problem.

Do stay current on existing accounts – Late payments on your existing mortgage, car payment, or anything else that can be reported to a Credit Reporting Agencies can cost you dearly. One 30-day late payment can cost anywhere from 30 to 75 points on your credit score.

Do continue to use your credit as you normally would – Red flags are easily raised within the scoring system. If it appears you are diverting from your normal spending patterns, it could cause your score to go down. For example, if you've had a monthly service for Internet access billed to the same credit card for the past three years, there's really no reason to drop it now. Again, make your changes after the loan funds.

Do call your Loan Consultant – If you receive notification from a collection agency or creditor that could potentially have an adverse effect on your credit score, call your loan consultant so that he can try to direct you to the right resources and prevent any derogatory reporting to credit bureaus.

SOURCE: Based on The Top 10 Credit Do's and Don'ts during the Loan Process, provided by Credit Resource Corp. http://www.creditresourcecorp.com

Email me and I will send you a Consumer Credit Scoring Booklet with a ton of good information on Credit Scoring.

"People usually are the happiest at home."

William Shakespeare

Appraisal

One of the most critical parts of getting a mortgage is Appraisal. The purpose of an appraisal is to confirm the sales price for the lender.

What is an Appraisal?

An appraisal is a professional estimate of the value of the property that you are planning to purchase. The person who does the appraisal is called an appraiser.

Why do we need appraisal?

Lenders always require a home appraisal before they will issue a mortgage. They do this to protect their investment: if the actual market value of the property is lower than the sales price, and you default on your mortgage, the lender won't be able to sell the property for enough money to cover the loan.

Ask for a Copy:

While you pay for the appraisal, it is done to protect the lender, not you the buyer, and the report is usually sent directly to the lender. You can request a copy be sent to you as well, but it doesn't always happen automatically so you have to ask for it.

Cost & Time:

It usually costs between $350-$550 for an appraisal, depending on your property type and location. More expensive homes or homes that have more than 1 unit cost higher to get appraised. The appraisal process usually takes anything between 3-10 business days. The appraiser sends the report to the mortgage lender, but you have a right to receive a copy of the appraisal report if you have paid for it.

How does the appraiser arrive at the property value?

The most important component in arriving at the value is what is called comparable sales (or comps in short). These are similar properties usually located within a mile and have sold in last 90 days. The appraiser compares mainly the below features of the property against the comparables to arrive at the value

- Square footage
- Appearance
- Amenities
- Condition

So a large 4 bedroom home in an area where mostly 3 bedroom homes have recently sold will have a higher value, and a house with peeling paint and a patchy lawn in a well-manicured suburb will appraise at a lower amount than otherwise similar properties.

FAQ **What if the property appraises for less than the sales price?**

While deciding your loan amount as a percentage of property price, the lender will pick the lower of the Sales Price or Appraised Value. So if the property appraises at same or higher than the sales price, you could still get the same loan amount you applied for, but if it appraises for less, the lender will reduce the loan amount to match the value of the home according to the appraisal.

Though it can cause everyone involved in the transaction to panic; note that there are several options for the deal to still happen. If you wrote your offer contract to include a contingency requiring the property to be valued at the selling price or higher, you can:

- Walk away from the deal
- Negotiate with the seller to reduce the selling price
- Put more money down to cover the difference between appraised value and the selling price

- Request another appraisal: the lender may send another appraiser, or ask the original appraiser to review their report

- Dispute the appraisal: find out what comparable sales were used and ask your agent if they are appropriate, often your agent will be more familiar with the area than the appraiser and can find additional comps to support a higher valuation.

"A comfortable house is a great source of happiness. It ranks immediately after health and a good conscience."

Sydney Smith

Homeowner's Insurance

Most lenders will require that you have homeowners insurance in place before the closing. This can also be called hazard insurance because it covers natural disasters like fire and storms, and theft.

Why do you need insurance for a house?

Basically, the lender won't fund the loan on a property that isn't insured, and the lender will often require certain types of insurance and at a specific financial level (usually at least the amount of cost of replacement) to make sure they won't lose their money in the event of a disaster.

Also, depending on the geographic area you may need to carry specific types of insurance, like earthquake or flood insurance.

Types of Coverage: Most insurance policies have several sections, each one covering a different aspect of homeownership:

Dwelling Insurance: pays for damages to the structure of the home, outbuildings, detached garages, etc.

Personal Property: covers household items, including furniture, clothing, appliances and electronics which are damaged or stolen. (After an event, many people find that they have a lot more stuff than is covered in their policy, do an inventory and videotape your possessions.)

Liability Insurance: protects you against financial loss if you are found legally responsible for someone else's injury or property damage.

Medical payments: pays the medical bills for anyone injured on your property (and some injuries away from the property, for example, if your dog bites someone).

Loss of Use: covers living expenses if your property is destroyed or too damaged to live in while being repaired.

Flood Insurance: many lenders and some states require a specific policy for flood insurance.

Homeowner's Insurance: Put the Right Policy in Place

Experts agree that the most important question homeowners should ask when shopping for a plan is the A.M. Best rating of each company. New companies pop up all the time, and homeowners need to be informed about what a company can offer in terms of protection against potential risk.

Consumers should also become familiar with the liability portion of their policy. ACV (Actual Cash Value) policies pay claims based upon the depreciated value of the item or items lost. However, replacement cost policies will pay the full cost required to actually replace the items.

To ensure that the right amount of insurance is purchased, homeowners should obtain an appraisal every five years or so. If additions are made or remodeling takes place, homeowners will need to revisit and possibly upgrade their plan as well.

Experts say there are several important mistakes homeowners should be especially careful to avoid. The first is being dishonest on an application. This is absolute grounds to reject any claim. Secondly, if the property contains a detached structure - such as a guest house, a barn, a workshop, or a garage - be sure to include each one on the insurance policy. Finally, do not over-insure. Homeowners can save a little money by insuring only those items and structures that need to be replaced.

"Home is where there's one to love us."

Charles Swain

Home Warranty

For many new owners, this is a great way to gain peace of mind about problems that they used to call the landlord to fix: ones that often aren't covered under their homeowner's insurance.

But you need to read your contract carefully to see what is covered, and make sure the company offering the warranty will fix water heater when it breaks on a wintry Saturday midnight.

Two Types of Coverage: New Homes and Pre-Owned

Pre-Owned Home Warranties: covers normal wear and tear, but not major pre-existing conditions, usually offered in homes 5 years and older.

Cost: usually between $250 and $600/year, with deductibles of $25-$100, and service fees ranging from $10-100 per call.

Purchased by:

Seller: to make the property more attractive and minimize disputes after the sale, or as part of negotiation with buyer.

Real Estate Agent: a common thank you gift to the buyers celebrating a successful transaction.

Buyer: In case both seller and Real Estate Agent don't pay, it may be a good idea to get a Home Warranty at least for the first year.

Renewal: Most policies are renewable at the end of the year.

New Home Warranties: Are purchased by the developer and they can last for as long as 10 years. It usually covers the roof, structure, and foundation. Add-on coverage can include construction workmanship, materials and the home's mechanical systems.

How It Works:

An appliance or system of your home that is covered under the warranty breaks.

You call the company that manages the warranty.

They send a pre-screened serviceman (plumber, electrician, air conditioner repairman, etc.) to fix the problem or replace the appliance.

You are charged a standard service call fee, regardless of the cost of the repair.

When your original warranty expires (or one year after buying a home), you can extend your policy another year with the same company, or sign you up for a new one.

How to choose a Home Warranty company?

Make sure you are working with a reputable company (check the Better Business Bureau for complaints) and ask:

- How long has it been in business?
- How claims are handled?
- The company's financial condition

"Home interprets heaven. Home is heaven for beginners."

Charles H Parkhurst

Common ways to hold title

Title to real property may be held by individuals, either in Sole ownership or in Co-ownership. Co-ownership of real property occurs when title is held by two or more persons. There are several variations of how a title may be held in each type of ownership. The following brief summaries reference seven of the more common examples of Sole ownership and Co-ownership.

Sole Ownership

1. *A Single Man/Woman* – A Man or Woman who is not legally married.

2. *An Unmarried Man/Woman* – A Man or Woman who having been married is legally divorced.

3. *A Married Man/Woman as His/Her Sole and Separate Property* – When a married man or woman wishes to acquire title in his or her name alone. The spouse must consent, to quit

claim deed or otherwise, to transfer thereby relinquishing all right, title and interest in the property.

Co-Ownership

4. *Community Property* – Husbands and wives who acquire realty in the community property states of California, Nevada, Louisiana, Wisconsin, Texas, Arizona, Washington, Idaho and New Mexico can take title as community property. Each spouse then owns half the property, which can be passed by the spouse's will either to the surviving spouse or someone else.

Under community property, both spouses have the right to dispose of one half of the community property. If a spouse does not exercise his/her right to dispose of one-half to someone other than his/her spouse, then the one half will go to the surviving spouse without administration. If a spouse exercises his/her right to dispose of one half, that half is subject to administration in the state.

5. *Joint Tenancy* – A form of Co-Ownership by two or more individuals (none of which can be a corporation, partnership, Limited Liability Company or trustees of a trust) in equal shares, by a title created by a single transfer, when expressly declared in the transfer to be a joint tenancy. The joint tenants must derive their title at the same time from a single transfer, share identical

interests and have equal rights of possession. On the death of one Co-Tenant the survivor or survivors take no new title but hold the entire estate under the original transfer.

6. *Tenancy in Common* – This is a form of Co-Ownership with two or more individuals or entities. The interest of each individual or entity may or may not be stated and may not be equal. A Tenant in Common has the right to deal with its interest as it sees fit - sell, hypothecate, lease, gift, etc.

7. *Trust* – Title to real property may be held in a title holding trust. The trust holds legal and equitable title to the real estate. The trustee holds title for the trustor/beneficiary who retains all the management rights and responsibilities. There are many advantages to holding title in a trust, such as avoidance of probate costs and delays.

Note that there is a cost of creating a living trust and deeding real property into the living trust. If the trustor becomes incompetent, the named alternate trustor (such as a spouse or adult child) takes over management of the trust assets. When the trustor dies, the assets are distributed according to the trust's terms.

The preceding summaries are few of the more common ways to take title to real property. For more comprehensive understanding of legal and tax consequences, appropriate consultation with your attorney and/or CPA is recommended.

"If you want a golden rule that will fit everything, this is it: Having nothing in your house that you do not know to be useful or believe to be beautiful."

William Morris

Moving Tips

Moving is almost never a pleasant experience. But if you are moving from your rented house to the one that you own, I am sure it's something to look forward to. Below I have included a checklist that will make your move a hassle free.

✓ Inform United States postal service of your move so that they can forward your mails to the new address. You can do this by visiting your local post office or online at www.usps.com.

✓ Inform about your address change to all your financial institutions, your employer, IRS, DMV, Insurance company, your doctor office, children school, newspaper & magazine subscription, and any other relevant service provider/company.

✓ Arrange to cancel utilities and services at your old home and have them installed in your new home.

✓ Inform your friends, relatives, and co-workers about your new address and phone numbers.

✓ Ask for a Mover recommendation from your real estate agent, loan professional and your friends & family. Decide on a mover at least 2-4 weeks in advance. Usually, good movers get booked for weekends in advance.

✓ Find out about local grocery stores, restaurants, cleaners etc from your real estate agent and/or any friends living in the neighborhood.

✓ Pack your first day handy items box separately so that they are handy when you need them. Try moving on a Friday so that you get the whole weekend to settle down in your new house.

"I have been very happy with my homes, but homes really are no more than people who live in them."

Nancy Reagan

What the First-Time Home Buyers are saying

To get you a real flavor of how some of the First Time Home Buyers felt before and after the home purchase process, I interviewed 7 people. All of them were given the same 3 questions:

1. What was the main motivation of buying your first home?

2. What are some of the things that you would have known at the beginning of the process that would have made your experience better?

3. Any tips/suggestions for future First Time Home Buyers?

Make sure you read this chapter very carefully. Lot of them came up with really useful tips based on their experience.

Kishan Ramaswamy

What was the main motivation of buying your first home?

- We wanted to own a place that we can call a home. Just needed the satisfaction of being in a place that you can call your own. You have the liberty and knowing that you have the liberty of customizing it the way you want. The joy of coming back from a hectic day at work to a relaxing home.

- There is always the fact of building equity. You have a choice of either paying rent or paying a mortgage that goes towards owning your own home.

- If you are like me, who has a 30 year fixed, you can be assured that for the duration of the loan, you are not going to pay a dollar more per month as compared to renting a place, where you are at the mercy of the landlord.

What are some of the things that you would have known at the beginning of the process that would have made your experience better?

- Always the tricky part is understanding the different loan options available. Need to thoroughly understand what an ARM is and the advantages and disadvantages as compared to a traditional 30 year mortgage.

- What exactly is the true value of the property? Sites like Zillow, Trulia provide you with a guidance, but cannot be taken for the true representation of the price. Knowing an accurate value of the property is a challenge and is difficult to know how much to offer.

Anything else that you would like to share and/or you would advise a future First-Time Buyer

- Always take your time in deciding the location. Your own home may be good, but if the neighborhood is poor, it is not going to help you.
- Never rush to buy a home. A lot of the times, you will come across a home, which may seem ideal for you. You may even feel, that this was the house you were looking for. My advice is to hang tight. Do put forth an offer, but at the same time, make sure don't over bid and get into a bidding war. Make sure you know your limitations and stay within them.

Harjeet Singh

What was the main motivation of buying your first home?

- To get more space for kids to grow in.
- To put my money at work for me rather than paying the rent.

What are some of the things that you would have known at the beginning of the process that would have made your experience better?

- One main thing I should have known first was that for an FHA loan the bank (underwriters) want all Section 1 issues fixed before closing. We had to scramble at last minute to fix issues which may have cost me half the price if done with more time on hand.

Anything else that you would like to share and/or you would advise a future First-Time Buyer

- The most important aspect is to find a smart Realtor who completely understands your needs and priorities.

Saurabh Mital

What was the main motivation of buying your first home?

- We thought the houses in the area we were looking for were very affordable; interest rates were historically low too.
- But most importantly we were financially ready to make a commitment of buying a house.

What are some of the things that you would have known at the beginning of the process that would have made your experience better?

- No matter how confident you are about your financial stability, the loan process can sometimes be very exhausting and you would be amazed how much documentation lenders require these days. Make sure you have all your documents in order and easily available.

- Never get emotional when bidding for a house, you might get carried away and pay more than what the house is actually worth. Be patient and you will get the house of your dreams.

Anything else that you would like to share and/or you would advise a future First-Time Buyer

- Do the math; find out all the expenses involved in buying a house in addition to the monthly mortgage. Make sure you can afford it and if it requires making changes to your lifestyle you should be willing to make those changes.

Nermeen Ismail

What was the main motivation of buying your first home?

- The first one is to be able to live in a space that we can shape to our own liking.
- Also to have predictability over the amount of money that we need to spend on housing every month. With rent you can never predict how much that would be in 30 years time but with a fixed term mortgage the variables are minimum.

What are some of the things that you would have known at the beginning of the process that would have made your experience better?

- Nothing really! We actually had a very good experience with our house buying process.

Anything else that you would like to share and/or you would advise a future First-Time Buyer

- We were lucky to have a really good & professional real estate agent. So one advice to people buying a house is to get an agent that is willing to dedicate some time understanding what you want and what matters to you and someone who is capable of helping.
- Really my advice to those buying a house is to consider the buying process as a project. Plan your steps and execute on time so that you finish on time. It is not really as difficult as some people make it sound like.

Prashant Honavar

What was the main motivation of buying your first home?

- The major reason to buy the first home was the affordable price along with the low interest rates and State & Federal tax credits.

What are some of the things that you would have known at the beginning of the process that would have made your experience better?

- It would have been a much better experience if the appraisal process was handled better. The first appraiser reported the property type wrong and undervalued the property. We had to switch the lender and also order another appraisal, resulting in delays and more cost.

Anything else that you would like to share and/or you would advise a future First-Time Buyer

- It is very important to understand the roles of every profession in your transaction just to avoid any kind of confusion and misunderstandings.
- Be sure to get very precise information about the home/community/neighborhood from the Selling/Buying agents and more importantly all the relevant financing information from the Loan Consultant.
- It is much recommended that you do a lot of homework via different mediums like internet, books and talking to friends & family who have already bought homes. This will equip you with the right information so that you are well prepared in the journey of first-time home buying.

Sachin Vinayakan

What was the main motivation of buying your first home?

- When I was living in an apartment, I felt I was throwing my money down the drain paying rent. Now, as a new home owner I feel I am investing my money rather than throwing it away and at the same time enjoying the luxury of living in my own place.

What are some of the things that you would have known at the beginning of the process that would have made your experience better?

- Having knowledge of what type of loans are out there and what would suit me the best. I was surprised that I could buy a bigger house than what I had assumed I can afford.

- Reliable method to know if a house you are interested in is worth the quoted price. I missed some good opportunities because I took time to decide if the price was right or not.

Anything else that you would like to share and/or you would advise a future First-Time Buyer

- Location and layout of the house are probably the most important criteria to decide on a house. But also consider commute as one of your criteria - Commute to work,

132

schools, shopping, restaurants, weekend activities, friends etc.

Rakesh Agrawal

What was the main motivation of buying your first home?

- Having enough space for the new born to move around.

What are some of the things that you would have known at the beginning of the process that would have made your experience better?

- Most important thing that you learn in buying first house is the bidding process. Bidding process could be very tense because the buyers already like the house and do not want to lose it. At the same time, they do not want to pay extra for it. After going through the process once, we understood that the real estate market behaves like an efficient market place. Things sell at right price - not more (usually) and not less (always). If somehow we had understood this from the beginning, we would have been home owners earlier.

Glossary

Glossary

Abstract of title

A historical summary provided by a title insurance company of all records affecting the title to a property.

Acceleration clause

Allows a lender to declare the entire outstanding balance of a loan immediately due and payable should a borrower violate specific loan provisions or default on the loan.

Adjustable rate mortgage (ARM)

A variable or flexible rate mortgage with an interest rate that varies according to the financial index it is based upon. To limit the borrower's risk, the ARM may have a payment or rate cap.

Amenities

Features of your home that fit your preferences and can increase the value of your property. Some examples include the number of bedrooms, bathrooms, or vicinity to public transportation.

Amortization

The liquidation of a debt by regular, usually monthly, installments of principal and interest. An amortization schedule is a table showing the payment amount, interest, principal and unpaid balance for the entire term of the loan.

Annual percentage rate (A.P.R.)

The actual interest rate, taking into account points and other finance charges, for the projected life of a mortgage. Disclosure of APR is required by the Truth-in-Lending Law and allows borrowers to compare the actual costs of different mortgage loans.

Appraisal

An estimate of a property's value as of a given date, determined by a qualified professional appraiser. The value may be based on replacement cost, the sales of comparable properties or the property's ability to produce income.

Appreciation

A property's increase in value due to inflation or economic factors.

Assessment

Charges levied against a property for tax purposes or to pay for municipality or association improvements such as curbs, sewers, or grounds maintenance.

Assignment

The transfer of a contract or a right to buy property at given rates and terms from a mortgagee to another person.

Assumption

An agreement between a buyer and a seller, requiring lender approval, where the buyer takes over the payments for a mortgage and accepts the liability. Assuming a loan can be advantageous for a buyer because there are no closing costs and the loan's interest rate may be lower than current market rates. Depending on what is in the mortgage or deed of trust, the lender may raise the interest rate, require the buyer to qualify for the mortgage, or not permit the buyer to assume the loan at all.

B

Balloon mortgage

Mortgage with a final lump sum payment that is greater than preceding payments and pays the loan in full.

Biweekly mortgage

A loan requiring payments of principal and interest at two-week intervals. This type of loan amortizes much faster than monthly payment loans. The payment for a biweekly mortgage is half what a monthly payment would be.

Bond

A certificate serving as security for payment of a debt. Bonds backed by mortgage loans are pooled together and sold in the secondary market.

Bridge loan

A loan to "bridge" the gap between the termination of one mortgage and the beginning of another, such as when a borrower purchases a new home before receiving cash proceeds from the sale of a prior home. Also known as a swing loan.

Broker

An intermediary between the borrower and the lender. The broker may represent several lending sources and charges a fee or commission for services.

Buy-down

Where the buyer pays additional discount points or makes a substantial down payment in return for a below market interest rate; or the seller offers 3-2-1 interest payment plans or pays closing costs such as the origination fee. During times of high interest rates, buy-downs may induce buyers to purchase property they may not otherwise have purchased.

C

Cap

A limit in how much an adjustable rate mortgage's monthly payment or interest rate can increase. A cap is meant to protect the borrower from large increases and may be a payment cap, an interest cap, a life-of-loan cap or an annual cap.

A **payment cap** is a limit on the monthly payment.

An **interest cap** is a limit on the amount of the interest rate.

A **life-of-loan cap** restricts the amount the interest rate can increase over the entire term of the loan.

An **annual cap** limits the amount the interest rate can increase over a twelve-month period.

Certificate of reasonable value (CRV)

A Veteran's Administration appraisal that establishes the maximum VA mortgage loan amount for a specified property.

Certificate of title

Document rendering an opinion on the status of a property's title based on public records.

Closed-end mortgage

A mortgage principal amount that is fixed and cannot be increased during the life of the loan.

Closing costs

Costs payable by both seller and buyer at the time of settlement, when the purchase of a property is finalized.

Cloud

A claim to the title of a property that, if valid, would prevent a purchaser from obtaining a clear title.

Collateral

Something of value pledged as security for a loan. In mortgage lending, the property itself serves as collateral for a mortgage loan. .

Commitment fee

A fee charged when an agreement is reached between a lender and a borrower for a loan at a specific rate and points and the lender guarantees to lock in that rate.

Co-mortgagor

One who is individually and jointly obligated to repay a mortgage loan and shares ownership of the property with one or more borrowers.

Condominium

An individually owned unit within a multi-unit building where others or the Condominium Owners Association share ownership of common areas such as the grounds, the parking facilities and the tennis courts.

Conforming loan

A loan that conforms to Federal National Mortgage Association (FNMA) or Federal Home Loan Mortgage Corporation (FHLMC) guidelines.

Construction loan

> A short-term loan financing improvements to real estate, such as the building of a new home. The lender advances funds to the borrower as needed while construction progresses. Upon completion of the construction, the borrower must obtain permanent financing or pay the construction loan in full.

Consumer handbook on adjustable rate mortgages (C.H.A.R.M.)

> A disclosure required by the federal government to be given to any borrower applying for an adjustable rate mortgage (ARM).

Conventional loan

> A mortgage loan that is not insured, guaranteed or funded by the Veterans Administration (VA), the Federal Housing Administration (FHA) or Rural Economic Community Development (RECD) (formerly Farmers Home Administration).

Convertible mortgage

> An adjustable rate mortgage (ARM) that allows a borrower to switch to a fixed-rate mortgage at a specified point in the loan term.

Co-signer

One who is obligated to repay a mortgage loan should the borrower default but who does not share ownership in the property.

Covenants

Rules and restrictions governing the use of property.

Curtailments

The borrower's privilege to make payments on a loan's principal before they are due. Paying off a mortgage before it is due may incur a penalty if so specified in the mortgage's prepayment clause.

D

Debt

Money owed to repay someone.

Debt-to-income ratio

The ratio between a borrower's monthly payment obligations divided by his or her net effective income (FHA or VA loans) or gross monthly income (conventional loans).

Deed of trust

A document, used in many states in place of a mortgage, held by a trustee pending repayment of the loan. The advantage of a deed of trust is that the trustee does not have to go to court to proceed with foreclosure should the borrower default on the loan.

Department of Housing and Urban Development (HUD)

The U.S. government agency that administers FHA, GNMA and other housing programs.

Discount points

Amounts paid to the lender based on the loan amount to buy the interest rate down. Each point is one percent of the loan amount; for example, two points on a $100,000 mortgage is $2,000.

Down payment

The difference between the purchase price and mortgage amount. The down payment becomes the property equity. Typically it should be cash savings, but it can also be a gift that is not to be repaid or a borrowed amount secured by assets.

Due-on-sale

A clause in a mortgage or deed of trust allowing a lender to require immediate payment of the balance of the loan if the property is sold (subject to the terms of the security instrument).

Duplex

Dwelling divided into two units.

E

Earnest money

Deposit in the form of cash or a note, given to a seller by a buyer as good faith assurance that the buyer intends to go through with the purchase of a property.

Easement

The right one party has in regard to the property of another, such as the right of a public utility company to lay lines.

Equal Credit Opportunity Act

A federal law prohibiting lenders and other creditors from discrimination based on race, color, sex, religion, national origin, age, marital status, receipt of public assistance or because an applicant has exercised his or her rights under the Consumer Credit Protection Act.

Equity

> The value of a property beyond any liens against it. Also referred to as owner's interest.

Escape clause

> A provision allowing one party or more to cancel all or part of the contract if certain events fail to happen, such as the ability of the buyer to obtain financing within a specified period.

Escrow

> Money placed with a third party for safekeeping either for final closing on a property or for payment of taxes and insurance throughout the year.

F

Fair market value

> The price a property can realistically sell for, based upon comparable selling prices of other properties in the same area.

Fannie Mae

> Nickname for Federal National Mortgage Association (FNMA).

Federal Home Loan Mortgage Corporation (FHLMC or Freddie Mac)

A quasi-governmental, federally-sponsored organization that acts as a secondary market. investor to buy and sell mortgage loans. FHLMC sets many of the guidelines for conventional mortgage loans, as does FNMA.

Federal Housing Administration (FHA)

An agency within the Department of Housing and Urban Development that sets standards for underwriting and insures residential mortgage loans made by private lenders. One of FHA's objectives is to ensure affordable mortgages to those with low or moderate income. FHA loans may be high loan-to-value, and they are limited by loan amount. FHA mortgage insurance requires a fee of 1.5 percent of the loan amount to be paid at closing, as well as an annual fee of 0.5 percent of the loan amount added to each monthly payment.

Federal National Mortgage Association (FNMA or Fannie Mae)

A private corporation that acts as a secondary market. investor to buy and sell mortgage loans. FNMA sets many of the guidelines for conventional mortgage loans, as does FHLMC. The major purpose of this organization is to make mortgage money more affordable and more available.

Fee simple

The maximum form of ownership, with the right to occupy a property and sell it to a buyer at any time. Upon the death of the owner, the property goes to the owner's designated heirs. Also known as fee absolute.

Fifteen-year mortgage

A loan with a term of 15 years. Although the monthly payment on a 15-year mortgage is higher than that of a 30-year mortgage, the amount of interest paid over the life of the loan is substantially less.

Fixed-rate mortgage

A mortgage whose rate remains constant throughout the life of the mortgage.

Flood insurance

The Federal Flood Disaster Protection Act of 1973 requires that federally-regulated lenders determine if real estate to be used to secure a loan is located in a Specially Flood Hazard Area (SFHA). If the property is located in a SFHA area, the borrower must obtain and maintain flood insurance on the property. Most insurance agents can assist in obtaining flood insurance.

G

Gift

This includes amounts from a relative or a grant from the borrower's employer, a municipality, non-profit religious organization, or non-profit community organization that does not have to be repaid.

Ginnie Mae

Nickname for Government National Mortgage Association (GNMA).

Good faith estimate

Estimate on closing costs and monthly mortgage payments provided by the lender to the homebuyer within 3 days of applying for a loan.

Government National Mortgage Association (GNMA or Ginnie Mae)

A government organization that participates in the secondary market, securitizing pools of FHA, VA, and RHS loans.

H

Hazard insurance

A form of insurance that protects the insured property against physical damage such as fire and tornadoes.

149

Mortgage lenders often require a borrower to maintain an amount of hazard insurance on the property that is equal at least to the amount of the mortgage loan.

Home equity loan

A mortgage on the borrower's principal residence, usually for the purpose of making home improvements or debt consolidation. .

Home inspection

A thorough review of the physical aspects and condition of a home by a professional home inspector. This inspection should be completed prior to closing so that any repairs or changes can be completed before the home is sold.

Homeowners insurance

A form of insurance that protects the insured property against loss from theft, liability and most common disasters.

Housing and Urban Development. (HUD)

The U.S. government agency that administers FHA, GNMA and other housing programs.

Housing affordability index

Indicates what proportion of homebuyers can afford to buy an average-priced home in specified areas. The most well known housing affordability index is published by the National Association of Realtors.

I

Income approach to value

A method used by real estate appraisers to predict a property's anticipated future income. Income property includes shopping centers, hotels, motels, restaurants, apartment buildings, office space and so forth.

Index

A published interest rate compiled from other indicators such as U.S. Treasury bills or the monthly average interest rate on loans closed by savings and loan organizations. Mortgage lenders use the index figure to establish rates on adjustable rate mortgages (ARMs).

Insurance

As a part of PITI, the amount of the monthly mortgage payment that does not include the principal, interest, and taxes.

Interest

The amount of the entire mortgage loan which does not include the principal. Also, as a part of PITI, the amount of the monthly mortgage payment which does not include the principal, taxes, and insurance.

Interest rate

The simple interest rate, stated as a percentage, charged by a lender on the principal amount of borrowed money.

J

Jumbo loan

A nonconforming loan that is larger than the limits set by the Federal National Mortgage Association (FNMA) or Federal Home Loan Mortgage Corporation (FHLMC) guidelines.

K

Key lot

Real estate deemed highly valuable because of its location.

L

Lien

A claim against a property for the payment of a debt. A mortgage is a lien; other types of liens a property might have include a tax lien for overdue taxes or a mechanics lien for unpaid debt to a subcontractor.

Liquidity

The capability of an asset to be readily converted into cash.

Loan-to-value ratio (LTV)

The relationship, expressed as a percentage, between the amount of the proposed loan and a property's appraised value. For example, a $75,000 loan on a property appraised at $100,000 is a 75% loan-to-value.

Lock-in:

The guarantee of a specific interest rate and/or points for a specific period of time. Some lenders will charge a fee for locking in an interest rate.

M

Maintenance costs

The cost of the upkeep of the house. These costs may be minor in cost and nature (replacing washers in the faucets) or major in cost and nature (new heating system or a new roof) and can apply to either the interior or exterior of the house.

Margin

The amount a lender adds to the index of an adjustable rate mortgage to establish an adjusted interest rate. For example, a margin of 1.50 added to a 7 percent index establishes an adjusted interest rate of 8.50 percent.

Market value

The price a property can realistically sell for, based upon comparable selling prices of other properties in the same area.

Modification

A change in the terms of the mortgage note, such as a reduction in the interest rate or change in maturity date.

Mortgage

A legal instrument in which property serves as security for the repayment of a loan. In some states, a deed of trust is used rather than a mortgage.

Mortgage banker

A lender that originates, closes, services and sells mortgage loans to the secondary

Mortgage broker

An intermediary between a borrower and a lender. A broker's expertise is to help borrowers find financing that they might not otherwise find themselves.

Mortgage insurance

Money paid to insure the lender against loss due to foreclosure or loan default. Mortgage insurance is required on conventional loans with less than a 20 percent down payment. FHA mortgage insurance requires a payment of 1.5 percent of the loan amount to be paid at closing, as well as an annual fee of 0.5 percent of the loan amount added to each monthly payment.

Mortgage interest

Interest rate charge for borrowing the money for the mortgage. It is a used to calculate the interest payment on the mortgage each month.

Mortgage term

The length of time that a mortgage is scheduled to exist. Example: a 30-year mortgage term is for 30 years.

Mortgagee

The lender.

Mortgagor

The borrower.

N

Negative amortization

A situation in which a borrower is paying less interest than what is actually being charged for a mortgage loan. The unpaid interest is added to the loan's principal. The borrower may end up owing more than the original amount of the mortgage.

Non-assumption clause

In a mortgage contract, a statement that prohibits a new buyer from assuming a mortgage loan without the approval of the lender.

Non-conforming loan

A loan that does not conform to Federal National Mortgage Association (FNMA) or Federal Home Loan Mortgage Corporation (FHLMC) guidelines. Jumbo loans are nonconforming. See also: conforming loan.

Note

A signed document that acknowledges a debt and shows the borrower is obligated to pay it.

O

Open-end mortgage

A mortgage allowing the borrower to receive advances of principal from the lender during the life of the loan.

Origination fee

The amount charged by a lender to originate and close a mortgage loan. Origination fees are usually expressed in points.

P

P&I

Abbreviation for principal and interest.

PITI

Abbreviation for principal, interest, taxes and insurance.

Points

Charges levied by the lender based on the loan amount. Each point equals one percent of the loan amount; for example, two points on a $100,000 mortgage is $2,000. Discount points are used to buy down the interest rate. Points can also include a loan origination fee, which is usually one point.

Pre-qualification

Tentative establishment of a borrower's qualification for a mortgage loan amount of a specific range, based on the borrower's assets, debts, and income.

Prime rate

The interest rate commercial banks charge their most creditworthy customers.

Principal

The amount of the entire mortgage loan, not counting interest. Also, as a part of PITI, the amount of the monthly mortgage payment which does not include the interest, insurance, and taxes.

Property tax

The amount which the state and/or locality assesses as a tax on a piece of property.

Prorate

To proportionally divide amounts owed by the buyer and the seller at closing.

Q

Qualification

As determined by a lender, the ability of the borrower to repay a mortgage loan based on the borrower's credit history, employment history, assets, debts and income.

R

RESPA

Abbreviation for the Real Estate Settlement Procedures Act, which allows consumers to review settlement costs at application and once again prior to closing.

Reverse annuity mortgage

A type of mortgage loan in which the lender makes periodic payments to the borrower. The borrower's equity in the home is used as security for the loan.

Right of first refusal

Purchasing a property under conditions and terms made by another buyer and accepted by the seller.

Right of rescission

When a borrower's principal dwelling is going to secure a loan, the borrower has three business days following signing of the loan documents to rescind or cancel the transaction. Any and all money paid by the borrower must be refunded upon rescission. The right to rescind does not apply to loans to purchase real estate or to refinance a loan under the same terms and conditions where no additional funds will be added to the existing loan.

S

Second mortgage

A loan that is junior to a primary or first mortgage and often has a higher interest rate and a shorter term.

Secondary market

A market comprising investors like GNMA, FHLMC and FNMA, which buy large numbers of mortgages from the primary lenders and sell them to other investors.

Servicing

The responsibility of collecting monthly mortgage payments and properly crediting them to the principal, taxes and insurance, as well as keeping the borrower informed of any changes in the status of the loan.

Survey

A physical measurement of property done by a registered professional showing the dimensions and location of any buildings as well as easements, rights of way, roads, etc.

T

Tax deed

A written document conveying title to property repossessed by the government due to default on tax payments.

Tax savings

The amount of money that the homeowner is not required to pay the government in taxes because he or she owns a home.

Taxes

As a part of PITI, the amount of the monthly mortgage payment which does not include the principal, interest, and insurance.

Tenancy

Joint tenancy - equal ownership of property by two or more parties, each with the right of survivorship.

Tenancy by the entireties - ownership of property only between husband and wife in which neither can sell without the consent of the other and the property is owned by the survivor in the event of death of either party.

Tenancy in common - equal ownership of property by two or more parties without the right of survivorship.

Tenancy in severalty - ownership of property by one legal entity or a sole party.

Tenancy at will - a license to use or occupy a property at the will of the owner.

Title

A formal document establishing ownership of property.

Title insurance

A policy issued by a title insurance company insuring the purchaser against any errors in the title search. The cost of title insurance may be paid for by the buyer, the seller or both.

Truth in Lending Act

The Truth in Lending Act requires lenders to disclose the Annual Percentage Rate and other associated costs to homebuyers within three working days of the loan application.

U

Underwriter

A professional who approves or denies a loan to a potential homebuyer based on the homebuyer's credit history, employment history, assets, debts and other factors such as loan guidelines.

Uniform Settlement Statement

A standard document prescribed by the Real Estate Settlement Procedures Act containing information for closing which must be supplied to both buyer and seller.

Utility costs

Periodic housing costs for water, electricity, natural gas, heating oil, etc.

V

VA loan

See: Veterans Administration.

variable rate mortgage (VRM)

See: adjustable rate mortgage.

Veterans Administration (VA)

The federal agency responsible for the VA loan guarantee program as well as other services for eligible veterans. In general, qualified veterans can apply for home loans with no down payment and a funding fee of 1 percent of the loan amount.

W

walk-through

An inspection of a property by the prospective buyer prior to closing on a mortgage.

warranty deed

A document protecting a homebuyer against any and all claims to the property.

X

No Entries in "X"

Y

yield

The rate of earnings from an investment.

Z

zoning

The ability of local governments to specify the use of private property in order to control development within designated areas of land. For example, some areas of a neighborhood may be designated only for residential use and others for commercial use such as stores, gas stations, etc.